ORPHAN with a CROWN

A true story of gratitude, faith, family, and the will to survive

By Reeser Williams
With Jennifer Williams

Reejen Ministries
reejenministries@sbcglobal.net

ISBN: 978-0-6923-8683-5

Printed in the United States of America

Contents

Acknowledgements

I wish especially to acknowledge my departed father, Papa Van, who lived by the motto, "Going where others don't, doing what others won't." Your love, determination, and sacrifice gave life to a hopeless situation. Your acts of kindness and caring heart spoke loud and clear, telling me over and over that I had value just because I existed. The life lessons you taught me were monumental in my success. Your unfailing example of Christianity taught me that anything could be achieved if we put God first.

To my departed mother, Momma Van, thank you for loving me. Your compassion carried me through the hardest times in my life, and your reassuring smile, encouragement, and gentle hugs nourished my soul. I appreciate your willingness to accept me into your home and for creating a loving environment in which I thrived. I especially thank you for your determination in teaching me the value of praising our Maker. Your love for music encouraged the gift of song in me and created a lifetime of passionate praise.

I also would like to thank:

My beloved departed birth parents, Justin and Alourd, and my adoptive parents—my departed father, Rick, and my mom, Sue. I could never fully express my gratitude. Your sacrifice, love, and commitment could never be repaid. Thank you for going above and beyond.

My adoptive siblings—Chasti, Chad, and Savanna—you each hold a special place in my heart. I am proud to be your older brother and am grateful every day that you are in my life.

My blessed and capable doctors and nurses who performed lifesaving procedures at no cost to me or my family—thank you. Your expertise saved me from the clutches of death.

The families that opened their homes and hearts to me—thank you. I learned valuable life lessons from each of you. By welcoming me into your homes, you changed my life. Your generosity allowed me to experience the American dream.

Our brilliant editors—Joanna Kneller and Paula Fleming—thank you for your labor of love, spending hundreds of hours editing this project to make us look good.

Tim Vaughn—thank you for your countless hours of design. Your creative ability has brought life to our pages.

The many family members and friends whose thoughtful comments and observations helped bring my story to print—Rick and Nancy, Angie, Julie, Debbie, and Karen—thank you for remembering yesteryears.

My wife's beautiful family—Henry, Pat, Lisa, and Marci—thank you for accepting me into the family. You loved me just the way I am, and for that I am forever grateful.

I would not be alive today without the support of the ministers, missionaries, and many people who faithfully supported Haiti Christian Orphanage. Your service to the Lord has made a difference. Thank you for giving of your time, talent, and treasure.

I wish especially to acknowledge my dear family. To Jenny, my wife—none of this would be possible without your countless hours of writing and your dedication to our family. Thank you for your love and support. To our wonderful sons, Justin and Ben, and our beautiful daughter Madisen—you all played central roles in being the best part of my life. Thank you for being remarkable examples. You make me proud, and I am honored to be your dad.

And most especially to God—my gratitude is unending.

Foreword

The divine "markings" of the Holy Spirit are extremely special. In essence, God says, "I love a generation so much that I will choose one to impact many." The reality of our calling is not that God chooses the one He uses, but that God chooses the people He plans to save, heal, or liberate. His heart for those people is the motivating factor behind the one He chooses to send them. We see this in the cornerstone scripture of our faith, John 3:16—"For God so loved the world that He gave His only begotten Son..." The "marking" of one is based on the "marking" of many. The choosing of "one" is due to the "calling" of many.

This amazing and supernatural "marking" of God upon a person, although a sacred honor and privilege beyond words, comes with a great price. The mark of God on one's life is given before being formed in the mother's womb. Places, people, challenges, struggles, achievements, successes, disappointments, and distresses all play a role in forming, shaping, fashioning, and preparing us for the ultimate purpose for our existence. Joseph had no idea how his brothers throwing him in a pit and selling him as a slave, Potiphar's wife lying about him, and years in prison would prepare him to be the second most powerful man in the world, ultimately putting him in a position to save the world and his family. Esther had no idea how being an orphan in a foreign land who eventually was chosen by the king to be his queen would set her up to save her people from total annihilation. Daniel didn't know how the overthrow of his nation by King Nebuchadnezzar and Babylon, becoming a slave, and serving in the king's courts would set him up to be the second most powerful man on the earth in his generation, allowing Babylon and the world to be introduced to the real God and the Jewish people to return to their homeland after 70 years.

For those of us who are called to a people, it's one thing for God to give you a word. It's another thing to become a word. When I think of Reeser Williams, he not only has a word; he IS A WORD!! He's a living epistle that should be read by all men. His life so demonstrates Abba's love and the power of God in utter hopelessness that anyone who sees him and his family today would stand in awe of the glory of God.

What you're going to read will be life changing and transforming. It will build hope and faith in your inner man. You will believe for the impossible and have confidence that GOD STILL WORKS MIRACLES!!

— Eddie James
Eddie James Ministries,
Ocoee, Tennessee

Reeser was six years old when I first saw him. He was a cute little tyke with big eyes and a great smile that was somewhat clouded by those terrible protruding tumors in his jaw.

I saw his father hand him over to my dad's hand, and up the stairs of the orphanage they came. I asked my father why he was taking in the cute little fellow. Normally we only took in orphans. Dad picked him up, held him close, and said, "I really don't know, Rick. I felt the Holy Spirit tell me to take him in. I'm really puzzled by it myself."

Do you believe you have a destiny written in heaven? I believe Reeser has been one of those "chosen ones" of God to carry out a specific purpose in the kingdom of God.

Scene One: Dad (Papa Van) and Mom (Momma Van) were to save him from the terrible ravages of disease that run rampant in Haiti.

Scene Two: Mom loved him so much she cooked him special food he could eat without biting those bloody tumors. He became mom's special son! He was now my little brother.

Scene Three: Dad got Reeser into the states and in front of greatly skilled doctors who could perform free surgery to remove all those bloody tumors and save his life.

This was our role in his Heavenly destiny, and we enjoyed every minute of it. Others would play significant roles in his life—as you will read.

This wonderful book chronicles the exciting stages of Reeser's life. Years later he makes a full circle and comes home to help the very people who originally saved him.

Warning! You will thrill, cry, laugh out loud, and thoroughly enjoy this book. Now, lean back in your big chair and let's go!

— Dr. Rick VanHoose, Pastor
The Cathedral, A Bible-Centered Church
Evansville, Indiana

Orphan with a Crown takes you on a journey of love. It is more than a story of a poor orphan struggling to survive, but rather a true testament of the power of compassion.

I met Reeser in 1975 while on a mission trip to Haiti. He was an 11-year-old who loved to imitate Elvis Presley and make everyone laugh. Reeser was a blessing, even in the midst of his own storm, He put a smile on my face. His passion for life and his desire for music immediately knitted our spirits together when he came to live in the United States and attended our church. Reeser quickly became an important part of our worship team, traveling together—leading worship.

Reeser is now one of the most authentic and powerful worship leaders I know. He is a man of integrity who has a passion for God and His word. God has greatly blessed me with a lifetime friendship with Reeser, his wife Jenny, and their three beautiful children.

His life story will make you laugh and cry; it will impact your life with hope and appreciation. Reeser is a living testament of how God's love can transform a life and proves that no matter how insignificant we feel, to our Maker we are priceless.

— Bryan Pace, Pastor
River of Life
Phoenix, Arizona

Preface

Orphan with a Crown is more than a title; it is a mindset. It is the ability through faith to see things that are not as if they are. Even though I looked like a pauper, I believed in my heart that things were going to change. To make progress, I had to imagine a different reality and believe that it was possible.

For as he thinks in his heart, so is he (Proverbs 23:7).

"Character cannot be developed in ease and quiet. Only through experience of trial and suffering can the soul be strengthened, ambition inspired, and success achieved."

— Helen Keller

"Others can stop you temporarily—you are the only one who can do it permanently."

— Zig Ziglar

"Don't let what you cannot do interfere with what you can do."

— John Wooden

"You don't drown by falling in the water; you drown by staying there."

— Edwin Louis Cole

"Adversity has the effect of eliciting talents which, in prosperous circumstances, would have lain dormant."

— Horace

Introduction

My father was a voodoo priest. As a child, I recall sitting on the ground with my back against an outside wall, watching as dust rose and lingered over our premises. Dad was stomping in the dirt with bare feet, dancing in a rhythmic pattern to the tribal ceremonial beat of the drums. His dark-skinned chest was bare, clothed only with bright, painted-on designs; he wore patched pants and a scarf around his head.

Several of Dad's followers were gathered around the remains of an extinguished fire. Hot, smoldering coals burned red as smoke bellowed through the air while the drums beat with an intensity that made my heart race as the tempo became faster. Dad stepped onto the hot coals and began walking—each step more pronounced than the last with seemingly no pain. He walked slowly, his eyes fixed, as if he was in a hypnotic trance.

The intensity grew with each passing moment as the drumbeat quickened. Next, Dad planted his feet in the black ash, pulled out a machete, and plunged it into his stomach, forcefully twisting it as he pulled it back out. Unbelievably, the sharp blade from the machete left no lasting marks or cuts.

People were dancing, and loud, guttural wailings echoed throughout the landscape. The dancers contorted their bodies and writhed, jerking violently with every beat while the spectators' encouraging screams grew louder. These spectacles continued until the participants felt content that their spirits had connected to the ancient voodoo gods.

I spent many nights lying on the dirt floor of our hut, hearing the rhythmic sounds of the voodoo drums and smelling the coals burning from the fires that engulfed the island landscape. Fear would grip me as I lay listening to the sounds of the Lougarou (witches) vibrating off of our makeshift metal roof and imagining the evil spirits roaming freely over our hut.

On quieter evenings, Dad would make a black-magic mixture that produced the foulest odor, permeating through the air and leaving a lasting stench. He would strip each of my siblings and me, submerge our little bodies into a bath of this awful substance, and then recite ritual sayings over us to ward off evil spells.

I also recall nights when my ten siblings and I would lie in the dark, unable to keep from laughing and giggling as we recalled the day's events. There were eleven of us lying on the dirt floor in our small 10-foot by 10-foot, one-room mud hut. Our hut was like many others around us, built with nothing more than some recycled material, mud, broken branches, and reused block. Most huts, including ours, had no running water or indoor sewage system.

Mom had made a bed for us out of torn up rags and old clothing, and she and Dad had a small cotton mattress in the corner of the room. We had no furniture, no bathroom, no kitchen—not even a blanket—but we had each other, and that made me happy. After all, in my four-year-old mind, that was really all that mattered.

My family was not so different from many who live on this impoverished island. In Haiti, there is a mixed religion of Christianity and voodoo coexisting in a cohesive unity, worshipping ancient African gods in the midst of a Catholic cathedral. Belief systems are twisted together and intertwined throughout Haitian culture, passed down from generation to generation. People say the place where I was born is the voodoo capital of the world and the poorest country in the Western Hemisphere. The struggle to survive greatly overwhelms the population.

On many of those dark nights, I could hear Grandma and several aunts as they made their way into our already full hut. They would sit in the dirt, their backs against the wall, just long enough to catch some shuteye. Struggling to survive, living each day as it comes, is like a tsunami of hardship. It has engulfed the island, and its people struggle to keep their heads afloat, gasping for air.

It's A Boy

My journey began in 1964 in Port-au-Prince, Haiti. I was born in late August to a woman who would come to have thirteen children. Momma had given birth to four others before me, but nothing could have prepared her for what she experienced at the time of my birth.

The day was hot and humid. Work needed to be done, and food was scarce. The sun was beating down with a vengeance, leaving only a small shadow where several people had gathered to rest. Even though she was weak and malnourished, Momma worked hard caring for the other children. She swept the dirt floor of our hut, carried water in large buckets on her head, and cooked small amounts of food on the open fire.

Despite being pregnant, her body was thin and frail. Her dresses were ragged and faded, and she rarely had shoes. Her skin was dry from the harsh sun, and she wore a tattered scarf to protect her head.

And then her time came. With no access to medical care, she labored on the dirt floor of our family's hut—rags underneath her as a cushion, the still air pressing around her like a wet blanket, and her sisters attending her—until I made my appearance in the world.

From the first glance, it was clear that something was terribly wrong. As Momma held me in her arms, she could only pray that God would somehow save her child, a baby boy she named Louissaint. As she held me up to the light that filtered in through the doorway, her heart faltered as she examined the hemangioma that engulfed my bottom lip.

Weak from the delivery and malnutrition, Momma rested from the day's events and prayed that in the morning things would be different. But as the sun rose and the days went by, my condition worsened. It soon became known that my tumor was a bleeder that would eventually prove to be life threatening. Since life was already difficult—little food, little shelter, lack of water, and no medical help—my parents were faced with the torment of family and community members' demands to throw me away into a hole dug for a toilet. After all, the life expectancy for 75 percent of healthy babies was only to the age of five, so how was I going to make it?

Even the task of feeding me became daunting and overwhelming. Nursing me was time-consuming and difficult, and keeping me from dying of dehydration and malnutrition was an ongoing battle. My mom was a fighter, and this was a fight she was not willing to lose. With a faith in God and a determination not to give up, she miraculously kept me alive. Even though Dad was a voodoo priest, Momma was a believer and knew that God could answer her prayers.

For the first four years of my life, as I grew, so did the tumor and the complications that went with it. Fearing for my life, my parents sought help and refuge at a distant Catholic clinic. Our journey began early in the morning over dusty, rocky roads, which we walked for miles. Momma stayed home tending to the needs of the other children. Since I was so small, wore no shoes, and had little water and only remnants to eat, Dad would carry me. Switching me back and forth between his arms, hoping they would not give out, he would press on. He knew the sun would soon rise over the mountain and shine down with its relentless heat. Dad would often pause, pull a handkerchief from his pocket, wipe my brow, and after a short hesitation, continue on. He held me tightly as he climbed up the large boulders that filled our dusty path. This treacherous road led us to the care I so desperately needed.

The clinic was a small concrete building, which housed a couple of cots and a limited amount of supplies. Being that it was a free clinic, many came here for medical treatment. Dad would stand in a line that wrapped around the small building while we awaited our turn, hoping it would not be long. With the sun beating down and having no more water to drink, Dad would sit me down in a small patch of shade. The wait always varied—sometimes fifteen minutes, sometimes forty minutes. But Dad never seemed to mind. He knew that without proper care, infection would set in and take my life.

My gaping, blood-soaked tumor would receive a cleaning and a small medical treatment, which consisted of ointments and fresh gauze, and Dad always left with a handful of bandages. Though the medical attention was limited, it helped lift some of the burden my parents faced.

Dad and I made this journey once a month for about two years, until it became apparent that more must be done if I was going to survive. Once they realized my life was hanging in the balance, Momma and Dad sought the counsel of the Department of Social Affairs, which required a journey of many miles through several villages and towns. Knowing the long journey that was ahead, I stayed with Momma while Dad made the journey out of absolute desperation.

My parents hoped this would be the answer they were looking for. Was there a place that would help their dying son? After meeting with several men, the Department of Social Affairs gave Dad information on a place called Haiti Christian Orphanage—the place they hoped could save their son.

The Journey

I remember it clearly, almost as if it was yesterday: the sounds of roosters crowing, dogs barking in the distance, and being surrounded by siblings, aunts, uncles, and grandparents who were saying their goodbyes. Our mud hut was always full of family and activities, but this day was different. It was early Friday morning, and the sun gently rose over the top of the hill, casting its light upon the dusty, smoke-filled air. Our village was beginning to buzz with the sounds and smells of open fires as neighbors prepared their meals. Momma had prepared some bread and sugar water for Dad and me, as she knew we would need the energy for the day ahead.

I only owned two outfits, and Momma dressed me with my best one: a worn shirt, a pair of pants that didn't zip, and shoes made from rubber. She gently folded and placed my other outfit in a crumbled brown paper sack. These were my only belongings, and I needed everything for the journey I was about to embark upon. Dad had taken a handkerchief out of his pocket, tied four knots in each corner and placed it on my head to wear as a hat. He knew that the day would be long and hard, and the way the sun was already beating down, it would be hot.

Since I was only six years old and faced a long journey ahead with my pressing medical condition, Momma was emotionally drained. She stood quietly for a moment and then, without hesitation, picked me up in her arms for one final hug. Her eyes filled, and she fought back the tears. For six years she had fought to keep me alive, not letting me out of her sight for fear I would bleed to death. And now, through her love, she had to let me go.

Her thin frame quivered as the tears she had tried to hold back coursed down her dark, worn face. Knowing it was my only hope for survival, she held my tiny, swollen face in her hands and kissed me goodbye through her tears.

Dad stood in the doorway, ready for the day's journey. I remember the way the sun peeked in from behind, reflecting light off his curly dark hair. He was small in stature—his clothes hung off his frame, as if they were a size too big. He was a hard-working man whose hands were worn and callused from building and laying blocks; his skin was leathered and dry from the sun.

As I looked up at the figure in the doorway, my mind went to yesterdays when Dad would wake before dawn. He would work a ten-hour day, making only $1.50. Dad was always faithful with the money he earned, which was just enough to bring home rice and beans for dinner. Momma would eagerly await his arrival, prepared with a fire and a large pot. I remember the smell of onions and special spices sautéing over the open fire as I waited for Momma to finish cooking the meal. We would sit together on the dirt ground waiting excitedly for Momma to pile the rice and beans onto a large dish. Dad would always take the first couple of bites and then hand the plate to Momma. She would do the same, and then she would feed us kids. I never remember my dad eating more than just a few bites. "I'm full," he would say, leaving the rest for Momma and us.

As I regained focus on the thin figure in the doorway, my heart became overwhelmed. This was my family, my home, and the only life I knew. My heart began to race with fear of the unknown. How would we make the trip? With little money and only a glimpse of hope—a hope called Haiti Christian Orphanage—Dad and I started our journey.

The sun shone brightly on the road ahead, which stretched, long and rocky, down through the village with discarded garbage on both sides and a thin layer of dust that seemed to infiltrate the surrounding air. Dad held my tiny hand in his as we began to walk. Momma stood in the doorway watching as we took each step of this well-traveled road, my many siblings standing by her side wishing us well. As tears poured down her face, I could only imagine what was going through her mind. Was she thinking this would be the last time she would see me? Was she wondering if they could help? Would I survive the journey? Or was she praying that God, with His mighty hand, would somehow have mercy on us? Would He hear a mother's cry?

As we walked, tears poured down my face as well. I looked back to catch one last glimpse of Momma, but soon I could no longer see the familiar surroundings. After a while, my smooth, brown skin became chalky from the dust-covered road, and my eyes were red. Merchants lined the road, sitting on the ground selling fruit, spices, and woven baskets. Women were adorned with colorful headscarves and balanced large buckets filled with needed supplies.

We lived in a remote part of Haiti called Carrefour, which meant we had to walk more than six miles before catching a taptap (Haitian taxi) in Port-au-Prince. As we got closer to the larger city, the road became more congested with merchants, bicycles, and vehicles. Cars were honking, people were yelling, and music was playing. This was very different from my small village in Carrefour.

Dad didn't have much time to let me rest, as he had to make this journey twice before sundown, and my legs began to ache with the challenge of maneuvering through the boulders that filled the dirt road. Dad only had enough money for two taptap fares, so we had to walk as much as my legs would allow. Once we arrived in Port-au-Prince, exhausted from our walk and from having no food and little water, we were able to lighten the load and catch a taptap.

I looked up toward the bright rainbow of colors that covered the taptap's exterior, and my heart raced with excitement—this was my first ride. The taptap looked like a small bus with the sides cut out and rows of bench seats. People were sitting, hanging, and climbing on all available spaces. Dad jumped onto the taptap and leaned over to lift me up, and off we went. Vehicles and pedestrians filled the bumpy road. During our ride, horns blared, people jumped on and off the vehicle, and we made many stops and turns. People leaned over the side, tapping the driver's door to signal their departure. I guess that's where they got the name taptap. Even though it was hot and crowded, it was better than walking. After what seemed like an hour or so, we were on the other side of Port-au-Prince, and our ride ended.

We reached the outskirts of Petionville as the morning was fading into afternoon. With more ground to cover and a long day ahead, Dad and I set off once again. This time we didn't walk as far, and before long we were catching another brightly colored taptap. I sat close to Dad, holding tightly to his hand, as we made our way through the crowded streets.

The open-air markets flooded the congested roadways. Traffic had come to a standstill as the streets came alive with the hustle and bustle of the merchants. As the taptap crept along the path, my eyes darted around, taking in the overwhelming sights. Fruits and vegetables were placed in the dirt among discarded garbage, and fish sat in the hot sun for hours on end waiting for buyers. Children dressed in neatly pressed uniforms walked along the dusty roads to and from school. I heard the screams of a donkey as its owner demanded it hold the weight of another unreasonable burden. Goats grazed freely on the abundance of garbage. I saw beautiful galleries as artists lined their paintings along the roads in beautiful displays. The markets were filled wall-to-wall, making reasonable travel an impossibility. Although slow going, this ride was shorter than the last, we were on the other side of Petionville in less than thirty minutes. We had reached the end of our road and would need to walk the rest of the way.

The sun was beginning to sink into mid-afternoon behind the hut-covered mountains. Dad wiped the sweat from his brow and grabbed my tiny hand, and we hiked up a rocky road. Before long, the hustle and bustle of the city faded. We found ourselves walking a road less traveled, the trees outlining the dirt road with patches of lush green and the loud sounds of the horns receding into the background. Once again, my legs ached with the challenges of walking on the rock-covered roads, and my tummy hurt from lack of food. With no time to rest or money for food, we pushed through, and before long, we reached our destination.

A narrow road led to a large, white, two-story building that sat on a small hill overlooking a lush landscape. Broad, white stairs filled with children lined the main entrance. I could hear children laughing and playing as my mind raced with fear knowing that our journey had ended. We had arrived. This was Haiti Christian Orphanage, and this would be my new home. Would I ever see my family again? It was so different from what I knew and so far from home.

I gripped my dad's hand tightly, as if to say, "I am never letting go." My heart pounded, and I could no longer fight back the tears that poured from my tired eyes. Just for a moment, it seemed like time stood still. Thoughts of Momma's reassuring hugs, my siblings laughing and playing, and my dad's loving smile raced through my mind. I would not be returning to the comfort of my home. For the first time in my life, right at that moment, I purposefully imprinted in my mind all the precious memories of the ones I loved so much. Home was hidden deep in my heart, and that's where it would remain.

Exhausted from our long journey, Dad and I found a resting place in a garage beneath the orphanage's second floor. The sun began to set, the light of day barely peeking over the mountain and leaving a beautiful red glow. Not having any time to waste, Dad quickly talked to a young man who resided there and then turned to say goodbye.

Dad picked me up, held me tightly, and kissed my face. He gently sat me down and placed the little brown sack into my hand, and then he turned and proceeded back down the narrow road. My heart ached with the thought of being left, and within seconds I found myself running down the road toward him thinking, "He can't leave me here all alone!" Tears poured down my face as Dad once again walked to the enclosed storage area, sat me down, and told me to wait for the Haitian director. After that, Dad started down the road again.

I tried to wait like Dad had said, but within moments my legs were running as fast as they could. This time I grabbed tightly onto his legs, crying, screaming, and pleading, "Don't go, don't leave me, please Papa!" But Dad gently picked me up, made his way back to the enclosure, and sat me down. He wept as he glanced back for a final goodbye. I could barely see his thin, tired face through my tears, but I needed to see him clearly to make another imprint in my mind so I would never forget. I wiped my eyes as fast as my small hands would allow so I could take my mental picture. I never wanted to forget this man I loved so much. The dark curly hair, worn and leathered skin, the smile with large gaps, and the eyes that seemed to look into my very soul all made their way deep into my heart and left a lasting impression.

As Dad stood wiping the tears from his eyes, he paused and looked closely at me. His callused hands swept over my face, gently touching each feature. He hesitated, and then wiped his hand over my swollen tumor. Dad was making his mental picture, too, because he never wanted to forget, either.

As I sat there, an overwhelming sense of hopelessness, loneliness, and heartbreak poured over me. In my short experience of only six years, this didn't seem right, and now I was left to process it all on my own. By now I could only catch my dad's faint outline as he made his way back down the long, narrow road. A sliver of light still left its glare on the dusty road as I watched him fade into the distance.

I sat there by myself, my legs curled up underneath me and my head in my hands. I was positioned just right, hiding my tears and, most of all, hiding my tumor. I was alone, embarrassed, and hurting. My heart thumped out of control, reminding me over and over again of the anguish that engulfed me. As I sat there, the pain of being left nauseated me. It seemed like I sat there forever, but in reality it was only about thirty minutes before three distinguished men stood before me.

These men were different from anyone I had seen before. They had pale, white skin and straight hair that was parted to the side and combed back. They were dressed nicely and stood with authority. Fear rose up inside, and tears poured down. I had never seen a white man before, and now three of them were standing in front of me. In Haiti, there is an old tale about white men eating little Haitian boys for dinner. I figured with all the little Haitian boys still running around, these three white men were probably full.

The first man walked towards me, grabbed my hand, and

pulled me closer to where they were standing. He did most of the talking. His demeanor was gentle but strong. He wore a white button-up shirt, black dress pants, and black leather shoes that looked new. His large hands gently lifted my face toward the light for a better look. As I stood there, several of the boys gathered around with curiosity. “Papa, Papa,” they repeated in unison. I immediately felt his love and concern, not only for me, but for them as well. I knew that he would help me and that he was the hope my mom had prayed for.

The second man reached out and grabbed my face to examine the tumor protruding from my bottom lip. He was very tall with a large build. He leaned over, bent his large legs, and put his face close to mine. To get a thoroughly good look, he used both hands to grab my tumor and began to pull, lift, and twist it. I later learned that his name was Dr. Render, and he was a surgeon at the children’s hospital in Akron, Ohio, who specialized in operating on this type of tumor. What are the chances that, on the day I arrived at the orphanage, a surgeon from Akron, Ohio, who specialized in cases like mine would be visiting? Even greater than that, this was their last night in Haiti—one night later, and we would have missed each other. God’s timing is perfect.

The third man, Eugene, stood quietly, watching the events unfold. He also was from Akron, Ohio, and was a friend of Dr. Render’s. He was a kind man with a big heart and was a hard worker who just wanted to do whatever was necessary to make the orphanage a better place.

Dr. Render immediately realized the severity of my hemangioma and did not want to waste any time getting me the treatment I so desperately needed. My tumor was fairly large, about the size of a child’s fist. It was heavy and had turned my entire bottom lip inside out, making it impossible to close my mouth. It was also ulcerated and bled with the slightest touch or movement, causing me tremendous pain and discomfort. Chewing food and keeping it in my mouth was extremely hard and took a lot of time and effort. Even the simple task of drinking water was overwhelming. Speaking was also difficult, and not having the ability to form words left me frustrated and isolated. The inability to eat and drink normally, along with the complications of bleeding, left me extremely malnourished and weak, threatening my very life. Without help, I would die from either infection or malnutrition.

After the three men left that night, the boys showed me around. We went down a flight of stairs that led into a large, dark room with rows of wooden tables and small wooden benches. Boys were standing in a line in front of a woman who was handing out small bowls of pudding. Each boy grabbed a bowl and spoon and sat at a nearby table. I followed, grabbed a bowl, and sat down, too. I had never had my own bowl of food and definitely never sat at a table before. Everything was so different; it felt like I was dreaming. Although I was very pleased to have food, my stomach still felt sick, so I only ate a little.

When dinner was over, a few older boys led me back up the stairs and into a large room with three rows of iron bunk beds. I couldn't believe my eyes! There were about forty beds, each sitting against the concrete walls in perfect rows that outlined the room. A third line of beds ran down the middle. There were several windows, some of which had glass, others of which had only fragments. A small room with a toilet stood off of one of the concrete walls. I looked around, trying to take it all in. These were all firsts, as I had never had a bathroom, a place to shower, or a bed before.

An older boy led me to a bed placed against the wall, close to the bathroom. I sat in disbelief, my mind and emotions on overload with all that had happened. As I lay down, I could feel straw poking through the thin material of the mattress.
I couldn't help but think of my family. I missed them so much. My heart ached, and before I knew it, the tears ran down my cheeks and onto my new resting place.

It was getting dark, and having limited lighting, the other boys—ranging in age from five to 20—began scattering through the room preparing their beds for the night. The room quickly came alive with their chatter, singing, and roughhousing. I just lay there, listening to the commotion, trying to quiet my mind. My heart hurt so badly, and soon my quiet crying turned into loud, heart-wrenching sobs. It was a night I will never forget; it seemed to go on forever. Thoughts of my family and the pain of being left kept me up most of the night. No matter how hard I tried, I couldn't stop the memories or the tears.

The next morning, I awoke to large sunbeams gleaming through the bedroom windows. I watched as the boys jumped out of their beds and began rummaging through clothing and shoes looking for something that might fit. The room smelled of pee-stained mattresses because many of the boys had wet the bed during the night. As I lay there, I realized that I too was wet and should follow suit with carrying my mattress out into the sun to dry.

The boys had formed a line leading down a large concrete ramp and into a courtyard that housed a muddy pool. Mattresses were strewn about on large concrete ramps, small walls, and concrete walkways. Ladies armed with large washtubs, lye soap, and washing boards were busy with piles of laundry. A large clothesline, weighted with the boys' garments, hung overhead. Chickens and goats roamed freely, and the sounds of the roosters could be heard for miles.

After we carried out the mattresses and headed back into the building, we were met by the aroma of onions sautéing on the open fire downstairs. We quickly cleaned up our room and hurried down the stairs for breakfast. This time a large pot of hot corn meal mush (*mais moulin*) awaited our arrival. This was good for me, because it was soft and made the daunting task of eating easier.

After breakfast, the boys scattered throughout the orphanage grounds. I made my way upstairs to an outside area, where I met some boys who were about my age. The orphanage was set on fifteen acres of lush landscape. We had fields to play soccer, trees to climb, and bushes where we could hide. A group of older boys sat on the white stairs leading to the main entrance. Their laughter could be heard from the side yard where we were playing hide-and-seek. Bright yellow tile covered the floor of the entry porch, making it a perfect place for playing marbles and other games. A larger group of boys had gathered there to play a made-up game using sticks.

Before long, the air was filled with fragrances of spices, rice, and beans. Two women wearing pale cotton dresses and worn headscarves were cooking in the kitchen below. It didn't take long to capture our attention, and soon we were making our way back down the stairs for another meal. It was hard for me to believe I would be eating three meals a day. I had barely gotten one meal with Momma and Dad, and many days we went without. Since I had not eaten very much earlier, and my stomach was feeling better, I ate every last bite.

Within a few days I began to settle into my life at the orphanage. But each night, as I lay in the dark, I would cry. The desire for my family would once again dominate my thoughts. My heart ached not only from missing my family, but also from knowing how extremely hard life was for them. I wondered what they were doing, if they missed me, or if I would ever see them again. Sometimes I would sit and daydream, trying to picture their faces. I didn't want to forget them, but most of all I didn't want them to forget me. Eventually, though, I began to feel more at home at the orphanage, and the overwhelming pain of missing my family began to ease.

For the first time in my life, I found myself in the routine of going to school. Darryl, the Haitian director of the orphanage, had fitted me with a new school uniform. I remember marching around the orphanage with my head held high. Wow! I had a new light blue, button-up shirt and navy blue shorts. I thought I was really someone now. I didn't know how to read, hold a pencil, or write my name, but I was overjoyed and ready for the opportunity. I couldn't believe it! "I just might beat the odds," I thought. "No, better than that—I hit the jackpot!"

School was held at the orphanage each morning. We boys dressed in our school uniforms lined the front entrance. Papa Van, whom I had met on my first day at the orphanage, had sent musical instruments as a donation. One of our teachers, Max, was a skillful musician and spent several hours throughout the week teaching us the basic skills necessary to pound out rhythmic beats and melodies. We stood on the white stairs in perfect rows, watching as the Haitian flag was hoisted up into the air. All eyes then moved to the conductor as he lifted his hand, directing the band. Each boy would sing as the band played the Haitian national anthem. We stood at attention, and in unison, we recited the Haitian ⍰pledge of allegiance⍰. At eight o'clock each morning, the whole island resounded with the voices of children reciting the pledge and singing the national anthem. Traffic stood still, and people everywhere paused to show respect for the island's anthem.

Afterwards, we marched in single file, hands at our sides and legs lifted high. The older boys would march into a room off the entrance while we younger boys went downstairs for our studies. Since books, paper, and pencils were limited, it was much easier for the teachers to have us recite our lessons. Although Creole is the common spoken language, in school we learned French and used it for reciting all of our lessons. We sat quietly on wooden benches at a small wooden table, waiting our turn to go to the front of the room to answer questions from our teacher.

We had homework each night, along with information we had to memorize by the next day. The teacher would swat our legs for any incorrect answer, which motivated us to do our best. Every afternoon we gathered in small study groups, helping each other memorize the facts for the following day.

Weeks turned into months, and before long I felt right at home. I still missed my family, but the pain of being left and the fear of the unknown were subsiding. I found myself so busy with school, chores, and playing with the boys that I had little time to think of much else, and I started to feel as if the boys and I were one big family. We would tease, double dare, and laugh at each other. They would often poke fun at me, calling me "crooked mouth" or laughing at the way I ate. With fifty boys at the orphanage, there was never a shortage of teasing, laughing, or playing.

The older boys took on the role of caregivers. They looked after us younger ones, making sure we got to school on time, helping us with homework, and occasionally, making us shower. We shared a strong bond. We were survivors, each and every one of us. We beat the odds! We didn't have much—only a couple of outfits and no shoes, underwear, or socks—but we had something greater: laughter. Laughter seemed to be the thread that strengthened our home, and that healed and comforted us. God's strength lived in us, and no one could take it away. It was a gift from God, a gift that each of us held.

Papa Van's loving spirit infiltrated the orphanage. Even though we didn't see him often, we knew he loved us, and that gave us a sense of security. After a few months, being the faithful man he was, Papa sent money for my passport. How could a man who had only met me in a brief encounter be so kind? Why was his heart so drawn to us? I didn't understand why he cared so much, but I was thankful that he did.

My tumor continued to grow, and the pressure in my jaw was unbearable. Each night as I lay down, the relentless throbbing would overwhelm me, keeping me up into the early hours of morning. Tears would pour down my face as I begged for relief. Without pain medication or medical care, I would often find myself weak and wanting the loving comfort of my mom. But Momma was not there, and the only comfort I felt was the hope that someday this tumor would be removed. I often found myself sitting on the sidelines watching the other boys, since their rambunctious activities were too dangerous. Strenuous activity caused extreme pain, as blood would pour from my tumor. One accidental hit to the face could prove to be life threatening. I felt lonely and isolated.

Divine Visitation

The Reverend A. D. VanHoose had been a pastor for many years. He had a growing church, a loving family, and a successful radio program. But one afternoon some five years before I was born, after hearing reports of God using others in a powerful way in ministry, he desperately cried out to God, begging Him to use him, too. What followed was an experience that changed the life and ministry of the man I would know as "Papa Van" and began to answer prayers that hadn't been prayed yet for a child who would be born with life-threatening hemangiomas.

On that particular afternoon, Papa Van prostrated himself on the floor of his church office, pounding his fist into the carpet and tearfully pleading with the Lord to use him or let him go from his ministry. His answer was an encounter with God.

Papa eventually collected himself and began to head home for the day. But as he walked through the church to the exit, he heard footsteps following him. He looked around to see who was there but found no one. So he continued out to his car, the footsteps still following. The footsteps didn't follow him into his house, but after dinner he heard a voice outside call his name. After questioning his family and learning that no one else had heard it, he realized who had called him. He returned to the church, the footsteps following once again.

When he got to his office, an angel sat down in a chair across from his desk. He told Papa that God had heard his prayers and sent him to give Papa instructions. He spoke to Papa of a number of things, including a tremendous missionary development in his ministry. This ministry became the hope that I needed; before long, Papa couldn't keep his mind off of Haiti.

Papa knew a Haitian pastor, Reverend Joseph Paulceus, whom he'd met through the International Ministerial Association (IMA). Not knowing anyone else from or in Haiti, he thought Reverend Paulceus would be the perfect place to start his missionary efforts. However, since Haiti was so destitute and had few modern-day conveniences, communicating with the reverend proved to be impossible. So prepared with only a word from God and an overwhelming desire to serve, Papa set off on his journey, stepping out in faith that God would help him.

The temperature inside the church was a blistering ninety degrees, but the Sunday crowd wasn't bothered by the smoldering heat. They sat quietly, dressed in bright but ragged clothing, hanging onto every word their pastor spoke.

Reverend Paulceus mentioned a man he had met through the IMA whom he later visited in America. He was certain this man would help the island of Haiti, and he instructed his church that morning to pray that God would send Papa VanHoose from America. The congregation immediately began to pray.

Then Papa Van himself walked through the doors at the back of the church and quietly sat down while everyone prayed in Creole, their native tongue.

The only white man in the congregation caught Reverend Paulceus's attention. Suddenly realizing who he was, he pointed at Papa in total disbelief and shouted, "There's the man we've been praying for!"

And Papa knew without a doubt that Haiti was the place to which God had called him.[i]

In February 1968—while I lay in the dirt as a three-year-old, struggling to hang onto life—Papa returned to Haiti, an instrument of God who was preparing my refuge two years in advance. With Reverend Paulceus's help, Papa had already established an orphanage that housed about thirty small children, but he quickly realized that he needed more help if he was going to make a greater impact.

The day after Papa arrived, he went to speak with a

government official to seek help. He shared his story, how he had established the orphanage and how he wished to expand and take in more children, with the government's permission. This official decided that Haiti's president, Francois Duvalier, needed to hear this, and he arranged a meeting for that afternoon.

Duvalier, called "Papa Doc" because he had once been a country doctor, had been in power for more than ten years. He'd created a militia to serve as his private police, but it quickly grew to twice the size of the regular army. Several years later, a constitutional referendum made him president for life, giving him absolute power and the right to name his successor.

During Papa Van's flight to Haiti, he had shared with a couple of acquaintances who were also on the plane that he was hoping for an audience with this powerful president. He was told it was virtually impossible; they had been trying for two years. Yet that door had opened right up for Papa.

Papa Van was told he would have two minutes but certainly no more than five with the president. He went in and told his story to Papa Doc, who shared his concern for Haiti's children. Instead of lasting five minutes, the meeting continued for more than an hour! It concluded with the "president for life" arranging for Papa Van to see several properties the government could offer for the orphanage he wanted to start.

Papa Van had asked for an acre or two of land from the government on which to build. Instead, by the end of the week he had been given a hospital building that was no longer being used and sat on 15 acres of land, free of charge.

On June 22, 1968, Haiti Christian Orphanage opened its doors —and with that, Papa secured my future and gave me hope.

Within a matter of days, the orphanage was home to more than fifty boys; Haiti had no shortage of needy children. Many homeless children stood in the middle of busy streets and lingered outside congested markets in order to stop passing cars and beg for money. Thousands lay in the dirt fending for themselves, deprived of affection and protection. They had no access to food and were constantly under the threat of violence. Papa Van, with help from the Haitian government, wasted no time.

Papa loaded these children into vans and welcomed them into Haiti Christian Orphanage. It took no time for them to settle into their new home. They quickly soaked up the affection Papa Van offered and knew that within those walls they would be safe and loved.[ii]

Papa's Coming!

The sound of women's laughter echoed as the wash ladies sat outside in the courtyard. The thin women wore cotton dresses, and they wrapped well-worn scarves around their heads to protect them from the hot sun. Their hands were cracked and dry from working day after day, and their knees were callused from kneeling on the hard dirt-covered ground. Conversation and laughter seemed to propel their hard work as they washed our endless mounds of laundry.

The sun filtered through the windows, lighting up the room where we bunked. The room buzzed with anticipation. This was the day we had been waiting for—Papa was coming! It didn't take long for us to begin jumping with excitement, bouncing from bed to bed and waking each other up. We scattered clothes throughout the room as we rummaged around for something to wear. A line of little boys marched out the door with pee-stained mattresses balanced on their heads, placing them in the sun for a much-needed airing out. Older boys mopped the concrete floor while younger boys picked up discarded clothing.

It was winter of 1970, and I had lived at the orphanage for about six months. My passport had been completed. I was now waiting for Papa's return.

Papa and Dr. Render had worked hard to obtain my medical visa. Dr. Render, who worked at Akron Children's Hospital in Ohio, discussed my condition with several of his colleagues, including some from Harvard Medical School. The necessary operation would be performed without charge. The expectation of finally getting relief from the painful tumor was almost more than I could bear. Papa's arrival also meant my return with him for my anticipated surgery.

I was overjoyed about seeing him again. None of us knew exactly what time Papa would arrive, so we took turns being on "lookout," checking every few minutes to see if there was a telltale cloud of dust from his car announcing his arrival. We did not want to miss that moment!

Papa would be staying at the orphanage. He had a large room down the hall from the main entrance that had been made into an apartment, complete with a bed, kitchen area, and bathroom. It was nothing spectacular by American standards, but in Haiti it was luxurious. Papa's apartment was perfect for his usual one-week stay, and it was "off limits" to the boys. I figured he needed a place to retreat when he had fifty boys vying for his undivided attention.

It was high noon, and the aroma of onions, garlic, and other seasonings filled the air. We always looked forward to lunch, as it was the biggest meal of the day, and without fail, every day it was our favorite: rice and beans!

The cooks downstairs prepared food in large pots over a big concrete pit filled with hot coals. They worked hard, wearing out any decent clothing they owned, and each held a rag to wipe away the sweat.

One of the cooks, Simone, had lighter skin and large gaps in her teeth when she smiled. I remember her well because she was a praying woman. Many times I would hear her talking to the Lord downstairs as she cooked and cleaned.

Large wooden spoons were used to dish the rice and beans into small bowls. The ladies would fill our small bowls with a heaping portion of rice and beans, and place them on the wooden dinner table, and then ring a loud dinner bell throughout the grounds. We loved the sound of that bell!

Boys would come running from all directions and fly down the concrete stairs. The younger boys stood in front of the line, larger boys in the back, and when every boy was accounted for, an older boy would lead us in reciting the Lord's Prayer. Then we would walk quietly to our assigned seats.

Almost in unison, we would lift the bowls up to our mouths and shovel the food inside. There wasn't much talking; we knew we could talk later. At that moment, we were eating and enjoying every last bite!

After lunch, we scattered throughout the orphanage grounds to play. Some of the smaller boys, myself included, hurried toward the front of the orphanage, where we had a better view of the entrance. The older boys always put us on "lookout duty."

After huddling up for a good discussion, we made our decision: hide-and-seek. It was the perfect game to play while keeping an eye on the main entrance.

Many of the bigger boys thought a quick game of soccer would help pass the time. The soccer field was large with trampled, well-worn patches of sparse green grass. It sat directly behind the orphanage's two-story building, just a short walk up a small hill. It was a great spot to see the road—and Papa, when he came down it.

The wait was agonizing, and the afternoon seemed to drag on forever. We played for hours until the dinner bell rang around five o'clock.

The boys came running, sliding down the stairs and waiting in line to bless our food. This last meal of the day was usually corn meal mush or bread and butter. We never had much variety, but that didn't bother us. We knew the conditions in Haiti—many didn't even have food to eat. So we didn't complain; we were blessed, and we knew it.

Not wanting to waste any time, we hurried through the meal and then scattered outside to resume our games. The sun was starting to set, painting the sky with a beautiful red glow. This was the best time to play as the heat of the day was subsiding, leaving a more pleasant temperature. The older boys were now in the middle of their competitive soccer game, and we little guys sat around a big tree by the main entrance. We were still on "lookout duty," and Papa would be driving up at any moment.

Just as we expected, the sound of the engine and the bright headlights came barreling toward us. Each boy jumped to his feet, raised his hands to the sky, and screamed over and over again, "Papa is here! Papa is here!"

The main boy on "lookout duty" ran up the hill as fast as his legs would go, interrupting the soccer game yelling, "Papa is here! Papa is here!" At once, all fifty boys ran toward the car, jumping, yelling, clapping, and rejoicing. "Papa, Papa!" we yelled. We ran excitedly toward the car that was now slowly maneuvering down the rocky road.

Papa rolled down his window and held his arm out high, and we all grabbed at his hand. Before long, boys were tapping on the car, hanging onto it, and trying to get a good look inside. "Papa, Papa!" we yelled, our hearts bursting with excitement. We crowded Papa's door, wanting to open it, each little face fixed on the man we loved so much. We held our arms opened wide with the biggest smiles, trying to wait our turn as Papa handed out welcoming hugs. A few older boys were at the car's trunk, lifting out heavy luggage and carrying it to Papa's apartment.

Within moments, our band, which included mostly older boys, had formed a line up the stairs. Papa made his way around to the bottom of the stairs facing the band, and with the attention of this very important audience, they began playing their fanfare of songs. Papa stood listening with each hand full of smiling little boys. We gathered closely, listening to the music and celebrating his arrival. He was finally here—our Papa had arrived.

Papa settled into his apartment and spent most of the week conducting business. We didn't see him much during the days, but in the evenings he would sit on the front steps watching the sun fade into the valley below. The boys would gather around him, holding his hand, rubbing his back, and playing games.

We would laugh and giggle as Papa tried to speak Creole, pronouncing words incorrectly and making silly faces. We loved his comical gestures. We would sit there for hours watching him act silly as each of us danced around him trying to catch his attention. The sun would disappear too quickly, and Papa would retire to his apartment.

The week flew by, and before we knew it, it was time for the other boys to say goodbye to Papa. Some gave Papa pictures they had colored or something they had made him. He tucked the pictures into one of his pockets, gave two thumbs up, and said, "I'll be back soon." Hugs were exchanged, and we tucked in for the night, closing our eyes and laying to rest the week's busy events.

It was quiet and early. The world was still asleep, but in a few moments the sun would peek over the horizon, declaring the start of a new day. Papa's visit to Haiti was coming to an end, and I was already awake, wondering what the day would bring. Excitement had kept me up most of the night.

Papa had come quietly into my room, picked me up gently from my bed, and taken me into his apartment. He had neatly laid out an outfit: a new shirt, a new pair of pants, socks, underwear, and new shoes. I could not believe my eyes. All of this was for me? I could hardly contain my excitement. The outfit had never been worn! I felt so special and loved.

As I sat there, my mind raced to thoughts of Momma and Dad. This was what they had fought so hard for. This was their dream. I was going to America! Would I get the help they had so desperately wanted for me? Out of love they had given me up; their love was saving my life.

I slipped into my new clothes, hugged a few necks, and sat quietly on the front steps waiting for Papa. So many questions flitted through my mind. What would America be like? Where would I live? Would I return to Haiti?

Though some details were uncertain, one thing was very clear: I was going to America! That made my heart flutter with excitement I could hardly contain. I found myself laughing out loud—pure joy bubbling over.

The air was dry, and the sun shone down with a vengeance. Papa opened the back door of the vehicle and gently held out his hand to help me into it. I plopped down into the back seat and sat up as tall as I could, stretching my neck but barely able to peer over the top of the door panel. My eyes scanned the scenery through the window. I remember the trees going by, one right after the other. I had trouble focusing on the rapid movements.

My mind raced with anticipation about this new adventure. I

was riding in a car! I had been in a taptap with Dad, but this was different—cool air blowing on my face, large fabric seats, and windows that blocked the dusty air.

Papa drove patiently, weaving in and out among the merchants filling the streets. I watched the sunbeams dancing through the dust that filtered up through the air. Papa would occasionally glance back at me and give me a reassuring smile, putting his thumb up in the air, as if asking, "Are you okay?" I would give him a nod, reassuring him that everything was fine. Our little gestures seemed to work well, breaking down the awkward language barrier.

Papa parked, opened my door, and grabbed his luggage. I followed closely as we walked into a large concrete building. My eyes were wide open, taking in all the new sights. Crowds of people, luggage, bags, and security check points—so much to process. This was incredible! I could hardly believe it. I was going on an airplane! Even more amazing, I was going to America!

The line stretched out onto a concrete runway. I grabbed Papa's hand while looking up at the enormous jumbo jet. The sun reflected off the large silver wings, and narrow stairs led into the main entrance of this huge aircraft. Passing through the door, I caught a glimpse of a large control panel. Two men wearing white uniforms with matching captain hats were busy pushing buttons, looking at gauges, and talking into headsets.

Papa nudged me ahead, guiding me down a long, narrow aisle. Rows of seats lined the plane's interior with small round windows at the end of each row. I was filled with curiosity, wondering what I would see outside those windows. If I was lucky, maybe I would get a seat next to one.

Nice women in pressed white shirts with blue jackets and skirts, and pins that read "Pan Am" were helping people place luggage into overhead bins. One helpful lady looked down at me, smiled, and showed us to a row of three seats. I excitedly squeezed my way through and hopped into the seat next to the window. I sat up on my knees with my face pressed up against the glass. Now I could get a great view of the plane's big shiny wing and its huge engines. This was one of the greatest things I had ever seen!

Staring in amazement, I barely noticed Papa. He picked me up, sat me on my bottom, and buckled the seat belt tightly around my waist.

My heart thumped in my chest as the plane moved into position for takeoff. How, I wondered, could something this big possibly get off the ground, let alone stay airborne? My tiny hands gripped the arms of the chair as the plane began its race down the runway. The engine roared, and the sudden vibration took my breath away as it rushed faster and faster. Within moments, my small body was pinned against the back of the seat and I was unable to raise my head as the plane lifted off the runway. Higher and higher we climbed with extreme force. My body was still pressed against the seat, heart pounding, hands gripping, and feet dangling. I turned my head toward Papa to get some reassurance. He looked down, smiled, winked, and put his large hand over mine. That was all I needed. Papa always made me feel secure. Having his large hand over mine somehow calmed my fear.

As the plane began to level, I began settling into this great adventure. Papa helped me climb onto my knees to get a better look. Pressing my face up against the small, round window, I saw an incredible view. White, fluffy clouds surrounded the plane. Patches of bright blue sky peeked through the clouds, and I saw aqua water below us. Small clusters of mountainous landscape and tiny trees sat along the ocean below.

Soon a large metal cart came down the center aisle, and the nice ladies handed out drinks and plates of food. As they came closer to my row, I wondered excitedly about the large cans of soda pop. I had never had anything like this before. One of the ladies approached our aisle, leaned over Papa, and placed a large can of soda and a hot plate of food on the tray in front of me. My very own can of soda! Papa took the napkin off the tray and placed it in my lap. Then, Papa did the most wonderful thing ever—he poured my soda into a large cup of ice. Wow! I stared in disbelief for a moment, trying to rein in the thrill that was about to burst forth.

The aroma of cooked vegetables and fried chicken filled the cabin. I ate the chicken first, since that was a rarity for me. Even though it was difficult to eat with my tumor, I was determined to enjoy every bite. After taking a few bites, I grabbed my soda, lifted it to my mouth, and tasted the liquid delight. This bubbly bliss would not go to waste; I savored every last drop.

Suddenly the plane dropped, and my tummy was in my throat. Turbulence! Oh no! I grabbed the arms of the chair. My heart pounded as we hit air pockets and the plane made small sudden drops. Papa once again put his hand over mine, comforting my troubled heart. My ears popped and my heart raced as we made our descent into the Miami airport. Papa reached over, buckled my seat belt, and held tightly onto my hand.

The engines roared loudly, and I heard the landing gear descend. The plane plunged from the sky and bounced onto the runway. My little body jerked forward as the plane's brakes squealed to slow the speeding jet, bumping down the runway for a few feet before coming to a complete stop. We had arrived. I was in America!

As I sat there, my mind raced back to Haiti, and I prepared myself for what I was about to see. In Haiti, people believe that money is spread out all over the ground in America. I thought it would be an overwhelming task to collect all that money, but I was up for the challenge. The richest country in the world was right outside these doors.

I was determined to collect all the money my small hands would hold. I would fill every pocket, socks, and shoes—wherever it would fit. Somehow I would get this money back to Momma and Dad. My family needed me. Within a matter of moments, my opportunity felt more like my responsibility. In some unintentional way, I had now become their hope. Could I somehow capture this wealth? Or, more importantly, could I be the blessing they had hoped for? With all of this running through my mind, I stepped out of the plane and into the unknown.

The airport ceiling seemed to stretch up forever. Large, round pillars and tall windows lined the halls. People walked hurriedly, dragging suitcases behind them. I saw lines, moving staircases, check-in counters, white tiled floors—but no money! I searched everywhere but could find not even a penny.

Papa grabbed my hand and hurried me along. We had to go through checkpoints and check-ins to catch our remaining flight to Evansville, Indiana. Papa's beloved home was awaiting our arrival.

I stood in amazement while taking everything in. I had never seen anything so wonderful. The enormous structures were clean and new. Bystanders were freely using tables and chairs. Bathrooms had shiny chrome faucets and clean, tiled floors.

Well-dressed businessmen walked by with their polished shoes, fair skin, and smooth hair. Blonde-haired children clutched baby dolls and lollipops and grasped their parents' hands. I was very different from those who scurried through the hallways. I was an outsider traveling through a land of uncertainty.

The passing strangers spoke mysterious words. My inability to communicate my needs to those who crowded the moving walkways became overwhelming and exhausting. Nothing looked familiar. Around every corner was a new discovery. Fear with a hint of excitement swirled around on the inside.

Within minutes we were boarding another jumbo jet. As we quickly took our seats and prepared for another takeoff, I wondered about Papa's home. What would it look like? Would I stay there? Was it made from mud like my home in Haiti? Questions bombarded my mind—unanswered for now, but I would know before long.

Papa leaned his chair back, closed his eyes, and grabbed my hand. I rested my head on Papa's arm. My eyelids began to feel heavy, and the edges of the dark blue seats blurred with the patterned carpet. I struggled, trying to quiet the images racing through my mind.

Papa had had a long week. The effects of the hot, Haitian sun, the daily business meetings, and the boys' emotional needs had finally caught up with him. He sighed with relief; he was almost home. In only a few more minutes, Papa's adventure would come to a restful end—but I had the feeling that my escapade was just beginning. As I rested, the plane plummeted from the sky onto the landing strip. Finally, we had arrived!

We grabbed our luggage and stepped into a car that was awaiting our arrival. As we traveled through Evansville, the sky was breathtaking with its soft ribbons of orange and violet engulfed in the clouds above. Manicured lawns with big trees and pristine homes lined the smoothly paved road. I peered over the door panel and out the window, fixed on the sun ablaze with beauty, casting long shadows. I could hardly believe my eyes. Was the grandeur of this beauty real? Families gathered outside, iced tea in hand, watching as children romped through the green carpet of freshly cut grass. Children played instead of collapsing in despair after a long day of manual labor. Everywhere nature was praising its Maker.

Within moments, we would arrive at Papa's home. I was restless with anticipation, and I could hardly sit still. My feet dangled from the soft fabric seats as I craned my neck, not wanting to miss this spectacular display. The peaceful journey to Papa's home was not what I was accustomed to. The trouble-free road wound around freshly painted, white wooden fences. There was no garbage, no dusty, rocky roads, and no street merchants—only clean, calm landscapes filled with brightly colored flowers lining the drives.

To me, each house was a mansion; I had never seen such lavish homes. The longer we drove, the more my tummy fluttered with thoughts of Papa's house. I was pretty sure by now that it was not made from mud, and by the look of things, I figured it would be larger than just one room.

After rounding a corner, we came to a sudden stop. I quickly sat on my knees, boosting myself up to get a better look out the window. A light red brick home sitting on the corner of a busy intersection caught my attention. The brick was trimmed with white and pink accents, and iron chairs painted pink sat on the small front porch. A wooden fence enclosed a well-maintained yard at the back of the house, and lush, green hedges and colorful flowerbeds lined the front entrance.

I sat in disbelief. Could this be the place? Could this welcoming home be Papa's house? It was more than my mind ever could have imagined. It had glass windows, strong wooden doors, and clean walkways. It was the most beautiful house I had ever seen.

A side entrance led into a quaint kitchen where the aroma of bacon and fresh, homemade biscuits lingered. A golden canister set filled with flour and sugar sat on the counter, and a large refrigerator stood against a wall surrounded by light wooden cabinets.

No cooking on open fires and concrete coal pits. No dirt floors or mud walls. I stood, in a daze studying my surroundings, trying to comprehend the magnitude of this life-changing adventure.

A large, gold cat named Biggin was curled up next to the refrigerator, and a black frisky poodle named Bobi danced around our feet, welcoming Papa and demanding affection. Papa bent down to give the energetic dog a quick pat.

Beyond a beautifully set dining room table were large windows that looked out onto a lush lawn. Huge oak trees stood tall, casting their shadow through the windows and into the room.

Sitting on a dirt floor sharing one plate of rice and beans was out of the question. This was the good life. This was something greater than I could comprehend.

A cozy living room with a sofa and love seat was next to the dining area. I sat quietly on the couch rubbing my hands across the smooth fabric. It felt so soft and comfortable. A large, grey, stone fireplace filled the opposite wall, creating a warm, relaxing atmosphere. Such abundance was overwhelming for a boy like me. I was captivated and sat in total amazement.

Papa's home was so large and engaging; around every corner was a new discovery. Endless beauty took my breath away as I walked down the hall and into the bedroom Momma Van had prepared for me. The bed was neatly made with fresh linens, a light-colored bedspread covering the large mattress and fluffy pillows resting against the headboard. The fragrance of flowers filled the air—not even a trace of the odor of pee-stained straw mattresses. I closed my eyes and took another deep breath of the comforting and clean air. This was a world away from the dark iron bunk beds to which I had grown accustomed.

A dresser sat close to the door, and on it sat a beautiful lamp that could be turned off and on at will. I stared at the slender fixture, wondering how it could produce such a warm glow without having oil or a wick and how this small invention could light up the room.

I got ready for bed, and Momma Van lifted up the soft sheets and tucked them in around me. I lay my head on the silky pillow and fought my tired eyes, not wanting to miss out on any new discoveries. I lost the battle quickly, though, and the warm glow of the light blurred into the soft white wall as my eagerness gave way to pure exhaustion. Within minutes, I had drifted into a world of slumber.

Birds sang their morning songs as the sun peeked in from behind the curtain. It was a new day, and the aroma of bacon, ham, and homemade biscuits filtered in from underneath the door. I quickly jumped to my feet and scurried through the house, not wanting to miss the next adventure that lay ahead.

Momma Van was rushing around the kitchen, her hands white with flour. Last night as I was submerged in a sea of discovery, I had hardly taken notice of Papa's beloved wife. Her neatly styled golden-strawberry hair framed her oblong face with its high cheekbones, a fair complexion that had been powdered smooth, and a friendly smile. Her slightly arched blonde eyebrows rose and fell as she reacted to Papa's stories. Long, thin legs peeked out from underneath a light cotton dress.

She walked over to where I was standing, placed her hand on my shoulder and knelt down in front of me to kiss my cheek, leaving behind an imprint of her glossy pink lipstick. As she stared at me through large-framed glasses, her blue-green eyes reminded me of the Caribbean waters on a bright sunny day. I liked the loving attention she showed me. I had not had a mother's touch for months, so this affection was welcomed. She then laughed at Papa and hurried around the kitchen to prepare even more food to add to the mounds that already crowded the counters.

The house quickly filled with guests. Family and friends were chatting, laughing, and filling plates, piling them with the wonderful delights that Momma Van had prepared. Papa's son Rick and his wife, Nancy, were laughing as Papa retold some of his adventurous tales. Papa's older son, Deon, and his wife, Jan, were busy chattering with Momma Van as she put the finishing touches on the table.

Soon it was time to eat, and Momma Van set out the plate she had prepared for me: eggs with perfectly round yellow yolks and topped with peppered milk gravy, a generous portion of bacon and ham, and homemade biscuits with butter running down the sides and covered with a dollop of strawberry jam. It was a mouth-watering display and more food than I had ever seen in my life.

I sat for a moment taking it all in. Even as I began to eat, I was in no hurry; I wanted to savor each new, delicious discovery. And savor I did as I carefully placed each small bite into my mouth, chewing slowly to avoid disturbing that huge tumor.

The warmth and love of this family was obvious. Conversation buzzed around the table as everyone enjoyed the delicious meal and exchanged smiles and heartfelt glances, creating a welcoming environment. In no time, I felt safe and secure. I may have not been able to understand anything that was said around the table that morning, but I heard the language of love loud and clear. This beautiful family had invited me into their home, but even more than that, they had invited me into their hearts.

After hugs and goodbyes, Momma Van quickly scurried through the kitchen washing pots and pans and scooping leftovers into the dishes that sat on the floor. Bobi quickly ran to his dish with his tail wagging, licking up every mouthful. Biggin sauntered through the room, rubbing his side against the corner of the wall. His long tail waved through the air as he lowered his head, delicately lapping up each delicious morsel.

Papa had made his way into the living room and was sitting on the couch with his feet on the coffee table. He held a newspaper that covered his entire face, so I could only see his hands holding each side of it. I made my way over to Papa, sat down on the couch, and snuggled up to his side. At that moment the world seemed safe, and for the first time in my young life, I didn't have a care in the world.

I sat looking at pictures that hung on the wall across the room.

There were pictures of Momma and Papa with Rick and Deon when they were small children. I was intrigued with the family photos. In Haiti, family pictures were rare and sought after. It was such a treasure to enjoy these precious images of yesteryears. As I sat there, I couldn't help but think of Momma and Dad in Haiti. I tried to remember the images planted deep within my mind. Closing my eyes, I could picture them, standing there hand in hand, their dark, worn skin and small, frail frames, smiling at me. I paused and then smiled back, and for a brief moment in time, it was almost as if they were there. I never wanted to forget them.

Bobi must have finished his tasty treat—I was so lost in thought that I barely noticed when he plopped onto the couch and was sitting near my lap. I enjoyed his overbearing display of affection.

Sitting with Papa and soaking up the one-on-one time was the highlight of my morning. This was much better than sharing his attention with fifty other boys. I let out a huge sigh and settled into the cozy comforts.

Papa lowered his paper and walked over to a large, dark box that sat across the room. He pushed a button, and immediately bright-colored images appeared out of nowhere. What was this? Where did the people come from? I sat there for a few moments trying to figure it out. In total disbelief, I hurried over, dropped to my knees, and crawled under the large box. Nothing. I jumped to my feet, stood on my tiptoes and looked on top. Where were the people hiding? I was completely puzzled. Papa was so tickled he gave out a big belly laugh. Momma, hearing the laughter, walked into the room with a dishtowel in hand. They laughed as I stood in total amazement at this spectacular display of entertainment. It was completely unbelievable! I couldn't understand a word, but it didn't matter. I sat there for over an hour watching my first television show, trying to figure out how those people got into such a small box. It was completely mind blowing.

After the program, Momma Van set out an outfit and prepared the bathroom for a shower. I stood watching water pour out of the wall, run around my feet in a circular motion and flow down the drain. Steam filled the bathroom as I pondered this remarkable convenience. The warm water felt so relaxing. I lathered up with a washcloth full of soapy suds that Momma Van had prepared for me and watched as bubbles floated around, popping with the slightest touch. Soon Momma turned the water off and wrapped me in a big, fluffy towel.

In Haiti, I had only experienced cold baths on the hard dirt floor, in a dirty river, or from a bucket. My Haitian mom would rush us, worried that the water might be contaminated and cause a life-threatening disease. At the orphanage, cold water trickled out of a concrete pipe. I never knew that towels existed; we would either air dry or dress while we were still wet.

But this experience was pure luxury, and I was enjoying every second! Momma Van rubbed my dry skin with baby lotion, sprinkled my neck with baby powder, and helped me dress in another outfit. As I slipped into the new garments, I remembered my Haitian mom's ragged, worn clothes. She would have loved to see me dressed so well. If only I could share the wealth and rescue my family from the clutches of poverty. The mountain of hardship was too big for me to bear.

The cloud of steam had left the bathroom, and Momma took me to brush my teeth. I gagged at the taste of the minty paste and tried to hurry through the torturous task. Momma Van lightly combed my Afro, gently tugging through the knots.

And that was the moment I first saw it—a clear reflection of my face. Before then, I had only caught small glimpses in the water or on a shiny surface, but I had never seen anything like this before. Staring back at me was a little boy with curly black hair outlining a small, round face. Dark, smooth eyebrows framed my dark brown eyes. I had high cheekbones, small ears, and a pug nose. And then, there it was, sticking out and overpowering every other feature—my tumor, and my lip hanging down totally engulfed with this horrific growth. I stood closer to the mirror and rubbed my tiny hands over the enlarged growth. A bloody scab held together a gap in the tissue that had been stretched beyond capacity. I stared at the tiny face looking back at me and wondered who it was. Questions flooded my mind. Could this distorted face be mine? Could it be repaired? Would I ever look normal?

The face looking back at me shook me to the very core. Suddenly I feared the future, and the only glimpse of hope came from the man I called Papa.

The bright red letters *K-m-a-r-t* were spread out across the front of the large building we were about to enter. Momma Van grabbed a metal shopping cart and started walking down each aisle.

With wide eyes, I observed women pushing carts filled with items. Small children sat in the front of the carts with their small hands holding onto a red colored bar as their feet dangled freely. Workers in blue uniforms stocked shelves and ran the checkouts. A blue light flashed in the corner of the store. White tiled flooring stretched on forever, and huge light fixtures hung from the vaulted ceiling. I had never seen such an enormous shopping market in my young life.

A wide variety of new, shiny products arranged in nicely organized rows filled every available space—no cluttered street merchants selling used products here. I couldn't comprehend one-stop shopping in such a lavish building. As I looked around at all the merchandise, I wondered, Is it free?

I remembered how Momma and Dad would travel on foot for hours just to buy a small amount of rice and beans. They had to travel even farther to gather buckets of water. It was backbreaking work and sometimes required several trips—and we still barely had enough!

Momma Van rounded the corner to hanging racks holding bright-colored clothing. I gasped as my eyes darted around. The department was filled with hats, belts, shorts, shirts, and much more. How could anyone choose?

Momma Van held up several outfits. I knew she wanted me to pick out a few, but I was having trouble deciding from so many options—I liked them all. Momma filled the cart with underwear, shorts, socks, and shirts, making sure I would no longer have broken zippers, bare feet, or worn-out hand-me-downs.

As I looked around, I dreamed of sending my family many of these wonderful new discoveries. One item in particular caught my attention: a beautiful white dress. How Momma would have loved that dress. I closed my eyes and pictured her wearing it. I no longer wanted to envision her wearing worn-out rags. She was my mom, and I wished with all my might that I could share my newfound blessings. With my eyes closed tight, I imagined her thin frame standing there with the biggest smile on her face. The new white dress fit perfectly as it blew in the wind. This was the image I wanted to believe in. In my mind's eye, this picture was in full focus, and it made me smile inside.

Momma Van interrupted my daydreaming with the most impressive outfit yet. She showed me a pair of pants, a button-up shirt, and a hat. They were paired perfectly and just my size. Momma held the outfit up to me and grinned. Excitement bubbled up from deep within, and my little legs jumped up off the ground as my arms flew around Momma's waist. "*Merci beaucoup, merci beaucoup*, Momma!" I exclaimed. In my wildest imagination I never dreamed of anything so spectacular.

America was in fact a rich and blessed place. It was rich because of people like Momma Van, and it was blessed by being a blessing.

I stood there in complete awe, soaking up the undeniable love that came pouring out from Momma Van's nurturing heart. It captivated my heart and overwhelmed my emotions. It was the same kind of love that motivated my Haitian mom—the powerful love of a mother who gave me up in hopes that I might live.

He Touched Me

Over and over again, she made me practice. "Try it again," Momma Van would tell me. I didn't understand English, but from the way she was banging around on the piano and looking at me, I knew what she meant. After days of practicing, the special day was finally here: our big debut.

Momma Van had dressed me in a light blue polyester suit with matching socks and shiny black dress shoes. She definitely knew how to put an outfit together, and any son of hers was going to be dressed well. It was Sunday, and Momma Van always wanted us to wear our fancy clothes.

We arrived early. The sun appeared from behind the red brick church building, casting its shadow onto the roadway. Women wearing flowing dresses and high heels clutched handbags and Bibles. Men in tailored suits politely held the door as women and children walked into the sanctuary.

I marched my black shiny shoes down the center aisle. I loved the way they looked against the bright red carpet. Hard wood pews lined each side of the sanctuary, offering seats for several hundred people.

The church services were full of guests and regular attendees. People greeted one another with handshakes and hugs, and I usually received several kisses.

Momma Van sat me in the front pew, close to the platform. She often glanced over at me from the stage, making sure I wasn't being disruptive. My feet dangled off the pew as I watched Momma play the piano. She knew how to make the piano talk; her hands would fly around the keys, making it look effortless.

Papa started each service with the congregation standing and reciting the Lord's Prayer together. I was familiar with the prayer, since we recited it before each meal in Haiti. Although I tried to pronounce each English phrase, I couldn't form many words properly because of the tumor that held my mouth captive.

Energetic praise music resounded throughout the building. Piano, drums, and guitars played fast-paced melodies, and the congregation jumped to their feet, clapping their hands and singing along as the choir marched down each aisle. Their red choir robes swayed from side to side as they lifted their voices, singing the inspired lyrics with passion. Contagious enthusiasm permeated the sanctuary, and people raised their hands, praised the Lord, sang, shouted, and danced with jubilee.

Momma Van moved around on her piano bench, banging the keys and singing her songs, captivated by the praise. I watched in amazement as she closed her eyes and raised one hand, never missing a beat. She was just as good with one hand as with two.

After the triumphant celebration of worship, the service transitioned into "specials." During specials, either the choir or an individual performed a song.

This was the moment I had practiced so hard for. Momma Van walked down from the platform, scooped me into her arms, and placed me onto the choir director's elevated stand. I stood in the middle of the platform, all three feet, six inches of me. Momma handed me a microphone, smiled at me, and nodded. Her reassuring gestures comforted my jumpy nerves. All eyes were on me as Momma walked back to the piano.

My heart thumped as Momma played the first few notes. My dark brown eyes were fixed on Momma as she finished the introduction, waiting for her signal to begin. When she glanced up at me with an encouraging smile and a gentle nod, I took a deep breath and gave it all I had. Since I had difficulty talking, singing was double the challenge.

I had no idea what I was singing—Momma Van had taught me the song in English—but it became clear that my spirit understood the words. With each word that rang out, tears filled my eyes. Feeling an overwhelming sense of love, I drew my tiny arm up, reaching over my head. I sang, hand raised through the tears, as He—my Maker—wrapped His loving arms around me.

The title of the song *He Touched Me* rang out so true that day. I may not have understood the words I sang, but I am elated that God looked beyond my comprehension and saw my need. He reached out from the throne room of Heaven and filled me with the wonders of His love.

Shackled by a heavy burden,
'Neath a load of guilt and shame.
Then the hand of Jesus touched me,
And now I am no longer the same.

He touched me, Oh He touched me,
And oh the joy that floods my soul!
Something happened and now I know,
He touched me and made me whole.

Since I met this blessed Savior,
Since He cleansed and made me whole,
I will never cease to praise Him,
I'll shout it while eternity rolls.

He touched me, Oh He touched me,
And oh the joy that floods my soul!
Something happened and now I know,
He touched me and made me whole."[iii]

There wasn't a dry eye in church that day; the display of God's handiwork was evident. Through broken English and a blood-filled tumor, God poured out His love, saturating my soul and proving how miraculous He truly is. It went beyond poverty, beyond being an orphan, beyond a life-threatening situation, and beyond my inability, filling my mouth with praise.

Momma Van must have seen something no one else saw. Looking at this massive tumor and the difficulties it caused, she must have prayed for God's supernatural gifting to rest upon me—

and it did. That morning transformed my life as God anointed my mouth to sing His praises. From the heights of heaven's gates, He called me to lead His people into worship, and the mantle of praise rested deep within my soul. God opened my mouth and filled it with His song. Out of impossibility, the miraculous rang out in the voice of a six-year-old child.

I now was no longer just an orphan searching for hand-me-downs and leftovers. Standing tall in His presence, I became an orphan with a crown.

He touched me, and I have never been the same.

After the service, people crowded around and shoved handfuls of money into my suit pockets. The sweet people at Bible Center Cathedral were responsible for the orphanage's success, generously giving Papa money each month. They had supported me, prayed for me, and loved me before I had ever set foot in the United States. Without their generosity none of this would have been possible. I was overflowing with blessings—I felt important, wanted, and loved. Once again, love made provision for God's great miracle.

Momma Van's niece, a beautiful young lady named Angie who also attended Bible Center Cathedral, had spent a week working at the orphanage before I came to America. She was kind and friendly and had asked each boy his name. Because of my inability to speak clearly, the other boys often spoke for me. "Louissaint is his name. Louissaint is his name," the boys repeated.

Unable to understand the correct pronunciation, Angie had said, "Oh, Reeser is his name." I didn't mind the change; Reeser was what they called me, so Reeser became my name.

But on that bright Sunday morning, as members of the church poured out their love and affection, my name was not important. All that mattered was that I knew they loved and cared for me.

I lived with Momma and Papa Van for several months while we waited for the Children's Hospital to set the date for my surgery. Yves, another young boy from the orphanage who also desperately needed lifesaving medical treatment, stayed there as well.

It had been a long time since Papa had small children in his house, and now he had to entertain two of us. Momma and Papa did their best to keep us busy, but pastoring a large church and keeping up with two energetic boys left them exhausted. Rick and Nancy, Papa's son and daughter-in-law, had much more energy and decided they would take us to the zoo!

Momma dressed us in tee shirts, shorts, tennis shoes, and hats. We didn't know where we were going—the concept of a zoo was foreign to us, anyway—but we were excited, because we knew something fun was in the works. Yves and I could communicate with one another, but neither of us understood English. We chattered together, trying to figure out what was coming.

The day was perfect. A breeze blew gently, and white clouds gave just enough shade while allowing the sun to peek through.

Rick and Nancy didn't have any children yet, so this was to be an adventure for them, too. Excitement filled the air as we walked through the main entrance, the concrete walking paths lined with rich vegetation and blooming flowers. Parents and their children gathered in front of large exhibits. I was a little unsure of what we would be seeing, so I stayed close to Rick and Nancy.

We crossed a wooden bridge that was held together by rope and swayed with every step. Peering through the wooden slats, I watched beautiful, bright orange koi darting around in the pond below us, their tails dancing through the ripples. Eventually we made our way to a wire mesh enclosure housing a variety of birds with multicolored wings and long necks. I stared amazed as flashes of red, bright green, yellow, and orange took flight above me.

Before long, Rick nudged us along a narrow pathway to a big, glass case where a large snake coiled around a sizable branch. Its eyes were fixed, and its tongue slid in and out of its mouth. I caught that scary glimpse from behind Rick's legs, and my heart quivered as I tugged on Rick to get him to move on. I had seen plenty of snakes in Haiti, and this was one creature I did not care to see again.

Yves and I had never seen such exotic creatures, and our

eyes must have been as big as saucers as we peeked through bars and stood on tiptoes to get a good look at each spectacular exhibit of amazing animals. At times, Rick would lift me up into the air so I could peer over the block walls to take in yet another new sight.

Discovering new wildlife made Yves and me feel quite brave. After watching a tiger pace a well-worn path through its exhibit, Yves grabbed my hand, and we ran several steps ahead of Rick and Nancy and down a large incline. Once we turned the corner, we could no longer see them.

Moments later, Yves and I ran straight into the most humongous creature we had ever laid eyes on. We stopped suddenly in our tracks, paralyzed with fear and disbelief. Our hearts pounding in terror, we gasped as the creature raised its trunk, stood on its back legs, and let out a deafening cry that shook the ground. Within seconds, our little legs pounded the pavement as we rushed back up the hill. This was a matter of life and death! Rick knelt down, his arms wide open and ready to comfort us terrified boys, but we ran right past him, to the gate. We had had all the fun we could stand for one day.

Rambling out loud, Yves and I thanked God that we had escaped the massive clutches of that horrifying beast—which we later learned was named Bunny the Elephant.

It was June of 1971, and I was six years old. The small, private plane felt as if it was hurling through the sky as it hit air pockets and made small, sudden drops that left my stomach feeling like it was in my throat. It reminded me of the rocky roads in Haiti, only this road happened to be ten thousand feet above the clouds. I gripped the armrest tightly and glanced over at Yves and Papa next to me, wanting Papa's reassurance that everything was going to be okay.

My nerves must have gotten the best of me on this roller coaster of a ride, because soon I could no longer hold the painful urge to go to the bathroom. My brown eyes filled with water, as I could no longer hold the overwhelming pressure. Papa realized my dilemma and, being the wise man he was, quickly grabbed a plastic bag and helped me create a makeshift urinal. Just in the nick of time, Papa came to the rescue.

After resolving this major predicament, I leaned back in my seat, grinned at Papa, and held my breath as we descended into Akron, Ohio.

A man named Eugene picked us up at the airport. He had graciously offered us room and board at his home in Akron, and he would be caring for Yves there while he recovered from his procedures. Papa also would stay there while I recovered in the hospital, and then I would return with him to Evansville.

On the day of my surgery, Papa held my hand as we walked down a long, narrow hall. A nurse holding a medical chart led us into a small room, placed a paper bracelet on my wrist, and handed Papa a light blue hospital gown.

Papa helped me undress, slipped the gown over my arms, and gently tied the strings that dangled down my back. He lifted me onto the bed, and within moments, the nurse was back in the room. She stuck a needle in my arm and hung an IV bag.

Papa filled out paperwork and met with the doctors and nurses. Occasionally, he would lean over my bed and pat my legs with his strong hands.

I tried to stay calm, but my heart thumped wildly, my stomach fluttered with nerves, sweat poured down my back, and my hands trembled with fear. The anticipation of the unknown was getting the best of me. If only I could communicate and understand what was being said! It was times like this that I missed my parents the most. There is nothing quite like a mother's comfort, and I needed my mom right then. But I tried to put on a brave face and be strong for Papa.

Papa hugged my neck and gave me double thumbs up, and I quickly did the same. We both paused for a moment with our thumbs in the air, looking into each other's concerned eyes. His big, reassuring smile brought peace to my jitters as the nurse pushed my bed down the hall and into another room.

The doctors greeted me with smiles, lifted me up, and transferred me onto another bed. Warm blankets covered my pint-sized body. Nurses and doctors stuck round patches on my chest, listened to my breathing, and kept an eye on my pulse. Monitors, tubes, IV bags, and trays holding medical supplies surrounded my hospital bed.

Soon after arriving in this sea of medical technology, my eyes became heavy. The silver light fixture blurred into the white walls, and I drifted into a world of induced slumber.

My hemangioma was a vascular malformation—a cluster of tangled veins, arteries, and tissue. Ulceration made this abnormality extremely painful and prone to bleeding that at times was severe and left me feeling weak.

A vascular surgeon, along with Dr. Render and several other specialists, performed the surgery. Because of the high risk of bleeding, they had to delicately map out the paths of the vessels feeding the lesion before they could remove the abnormal tissue. It was vital to block off these blood vessels in order to prevent any uncontrolled bleeding.

The surgeons meticulously carved through the large tumor, removing my bottom lip along with the mass of tangled veins and tissue. They then carefully stitched and bandaged an incision from my upper lip to underneath my chin, and within several hours, my operation was complete. My lifesaving procedure was a success, and now I began the long road of recovery.

This entire miracle was performed at no charge! Doctors, nurses, hospital stay, anesthesia, medical supplies, and much more were all donated to save my life. These wonderful men and women made it their goal to help those who could not help themselves.

The nurse's sweet soft voice echoed in my ears as I opened my eyes, groggily trying to focus. She laid warm, soft blankets over my legs, raised the head of my bed, and checked my bandages. Her bright smile and gentle touch were extremely comforting.

Through my blurred vision, a familiar face came into focus: Papa Van. He sat next to me, holding my hand. I was so glad to see him! My eyes were still heavy, and I felt drained. Feeling secure now, I nodded off again, knowing that with Papa by my side, everything would be fine.

I stayed in the hospital for several weeks after my surgery. Every few hours nurses cared for my wound, controlled my pain, and monitored blood loss. A doctor came in once or twice each day to check my chart and examine my sore incision.

I only understood a few words of English, so the nurses used warm smiles and hand gestures to communicate. Each morning they came in armed with baby lotion and washcloths. They would wash me up, slather me with baby lotion, and dress me in a fresh hospital gown. Even though I still missed my mom and thought of her often, these wonderful ladies pampered me as if I were their own, and I started to feel like I had more moms than I knew what to do with. Nurses who were not even assigned to my care would sneak by during the day just to bring in special treats. I felt loved, and this helped ease the pain of not having my parents with me.

Papa visited for a few hours every day without fail, checking on my progress, making funny faces, and providing moments of entertainment. He would sit by my side as we watched *The Andy Griffith Show* together. He would laugh, eat snacks, and joke around with me. Each day I was excited to see him, knowing he would bring a sense of humor and a few hours of amusement. I loved him so much, and I knew that he loved me, too. He always made me feel that he had nothing better to do than sit by my side. I was his priority, and he was going to make sure that I recovered well.

For weeks I was on a liquid diet, carefully drinking my meals through a straw. I worked hard not to interrupt the healing process. The nurses helped me with the regimen of rinsing out my mouth, which I needed to do a few times each day. Keeping my mouth clean and the wound free of germs was the greatest task.

They gradually began giving me portions of soft food, and within no time, I was eating almost anything I was served. I still had limited mobility, but eating was so much easier without the hassle of the painful tumor.

Word of my progress spread quickly throughout the hospital, and before long, nurses were sneaking in McDonald's hamburger meals. These delightful treats were much tastier than hospital food!

These surrogate moms were working overtime to make sure that I was happy and healthy. It's funny how the simple things in life can sometimes make the biggest impact. Not only did these nurses provide medical care, but they also brought a sense of well-being. Their compassionate kindness filled my heart and eased my worries.

For the first time in my life, I was free from the hemangioma. If only my parents could see me now! My mind wandered back to the time when my mom and dad had fought so hard to keep me alive. I remembered the long walks to the medical clinic and the exhausting journey to Haiti Christian Orphanage in hopes that I might be saved. Would word get back to them of this miraculous event? Were they still concerned about their son? I prayed that they had not forgotten me.

Papa Van's determination and his belief in God proved to be the hope in which my family believed. My miracle had come, and from so many sources: doctors, nurses, pastors. It delivered me from the chain of physical limitation and brought me to a place of freedom.

By 1973, I had lived with Momma and Papa Van for two years. I was now eight years old and had recovered well from the surgery, and it was time to return home. Haiti was a place of hardship, poverty, and survival, but Haiti Christian Orphanage was like an oasis in the midst of a sizzling desert—a safe place in the midst of a world of chaos. Returning to my family's home in Haiti would have been overwhelming, but returning to the orphanage was fair and manageable.

My heart fluttered with excitement, fear, and anticipation. I was excited to see the boys at the orphanage, but more than ever, I was overjoyed to see my family. I missed them so much! I couldn't quiet my thoughts, picturing their faces and remembering our moments together.

As these thoughts flooded my mind, one in particular kept replaying: I wanted my family to see, with their own eyes, the amazing transformation. For the first time, my family would see my face without the disfiguring, life-threatening tumor. This is what they had believed and hoped for, and now they could rejoice!

I became anxious as we rounded the corner and made our way up the dusty road that led to the orphanage. Boys came running alongside the car as Papa held his arm out the window, the roar of their voices echoing throughout the grounds. To my amazement, I could no longer understand much of what they were saying. For the past two years, I had only spoken English.

Once again, I found myself unable to communicate. At times, tears poured down my cheeks as the other boys jabbered, my heart breaking with the inability to understand. What were they saying? Were they making fun of me? It was urgent that I relearn my native tongue before I was reunited with my family. This became my top priority, and before long I was chattering right along with the rest of the boys and ready to embrace the family I had longed to see.

It was mid-morning, and the sun peeked in from behind the trees that lined the front entrance, casting a soft yellow glow. The orphanage was buzzing with the laughter of some boys who had gathered on the front porch to play a game of marbles. I sat on the front stairs anticipating my dad's arrival. My eyes darted up every few minutes, scanning the main entrance so I would not miss his approach. Oh, how I had longed for this day, and it was finally here!

My stomach fluttered with a thousand butterflies. Would he recognize me? I was much taller than the last time he saw me. I had filled out and looked much healthier, thanks to Momma Van's hot homemade meals.

I reached my hand into my pocket, checking that the twenty-dollar bill Momma Van had tucked in it earlier was still there. I was thrilled that this money would be the biggest blessing my family had ever had. With this much cash, they would be able to buy food for several weeks. I knew that whatever I did, I could not lose it! I grabbed onto it tightly, grinning from ear to ear and careful to not let anyone see it. My heart leaped with joy at the thought of my dad's response to this much-needed provision.

I took one more glance toward the entrance, and there he

was, walking up the dusty road. I sprinted toward the frail figure and threw my arms around his legs, holding on tight, not wanting to let go. My dad quickly bent down and held my face in his hands, gently rubbing his callused fingers over the area where the enormous tumor once sat. Now, only a scar was left—a reminder of the great miracle performed. Tears of joy poured down his face as he held me in his arms, speechless with overwhelming joy.

We had so much to be thankful for, and more than anything, we had each other. For a brief moment, it seemed as if time stood still, and we were the only two people in the world. I knew he loved me; his sacrifice and determination told me that. He stood silently, looking at me, and in a quiet celebration, we appreciated the efforts of so many wonderful people. Because of them—despite overwhelming odds—I was here, and I was alive. We had made it.

I had packed a few belongings in a small paper bag for the journey back to Carrefour to see the rest of my family. I would be visiting for a few days and then returning to the orphanage. I hated the pain of missing my family, but the burden of providing for me was more than my parents could bear. I would receive much more at the orphanage, so we would have to endure the pain of separation. But for now, I didn't want to think about goodbyes. I just wanted to live in the moment and soak up the love from my devoted dad.

Overwhelmed with excitement, I quickly reached into my pocket and pulled out the money, holding it out toward Dad, shaking my hand back and forth. He grabbed onto it, winked at me, and stuck it deep into his pocket. I knew he didn't want to make a big deal of it since many eyes were watching. We both grinned as he pulled me into his arms, squeezing me gently.

I grabbed on tightly to my father's hand, and back down the rocky road we went. Before long, the dirty street overflowed with merchants, honking horns, taptaps, cars, and pedestrians. We weaved in and out of these obstacles, trying to make it home before sundown.

After jumping on and off of taptaps and walking for miles, we finally came to a road leading to a small mud hut surrounded by many familiar faces—faces I missed and loved dearly. One face stood out among the rest: my mom's. Her thin face was dark and tired. She had braided her hair, and small white ties held the braids in place. Her dress was worn and her feet bare. She held a baby on her hip, and other children stood by her side.

My heart pounded at the sight of her. I let go of Dad, ran the rest of the way, and threw my arms around her depleted waist. Momma put the baby down and leaned over, looking closely at the face that was once distorted. She then grabbed me tightly, placed a hand on each side of my face, and without hesitation gently kissed each cheek and slid her fingers across the scar that remained. Her expression was one of pure joy. Finally, her son was free from the life-threatening tumor. I could never repay her unfailing dedication to my survival. Tears filled her eyes as she raised her hands to the sky and shouted, "Hallelujah, *merci seigneur*, *merci seigneur*!"

Momma had prepared my favorites for this celebration: rice and beans with a tasty meat sauce. We laughed, told stories, and rejoiced. Family and friends gathered around, listening as my parents retold the story of our miracle.

Sounds of delight echoed throughout the village as it came alive with curiosity. Word spread quickly, and in no time, our community rallied together, sharing in the joy of this remarkable event. In this sea of hardship, I stood there for a fleeting moment as a sign of hope—hope that transcended our circumstances, shouting loud and clear that we were not a forgotten people in a throwaway land. Hope came through a boy—the boy everyone wanted to throw by the wayside—and his miracle. Someone cared; someone heard our cries.

This was a night like no other. Everyone forgot the daily demands of poverty as triumphant jubilation replaced despair. On this night, they weren't just keeping their heads afloat gasping for air; they were standing on a mountain. My seemingly impossible situation had proven, right before their eyes, that nothing is impossible if we will just believe.

The Church

The Haiti Christian Orphanage had been open for six years, and I had now been back there for several months. Papa Van provided schooling, food, shelter, and clothing. By everyone's standards, the orphanage was a success. However, a dark shadow hung over the boys at the orphanage and the surrounding community: voodoo. It was like a coiled snake, waiting anxiously for its opportunity to strike. It lingered outside the orphanage gates, lurking around to infiltrate our belief system and poison our minds. The shadow of evil hovered like a blanket over the impoverished island, casting its spell. With its influence hanging around every corner, Papa knew it was time to build a church.

A voodoo temple stood just down the hill, not far from the orphanage, and a well-known and feared priest held services there. He would beat drums throughout the night, casting his spells. Many of us boys often lay awake in the darkness listening to the evil spirits tilling the ground. The pounding of iron hoes and scraping of metal rakes as they broke through the hard, rocky yard right outside our property haunted my mind. I remember covering my head in fear as the priest's evil powers roamed just outside our gates.

Edgar and Syvill Hudson, good friends of Papa Van's, took on the daunting task of establishing the building project. Thanks to their dedication, Papa's dream of building a church on the orphanage grounds was becoming a reality. The Hudsons moved to Haiti for several years and served as our American directors while they oversaw the project.

Papa Hudson was a large man who stood over six feet tall

and had short, straight, dark hair that he wore slicked back. He had a strong belief in the power of God, and he loved us boys, always standing for what was right and teaching us the principles of the Bible.

Momma Hudson was a petite woman with a smooth, porcelain complexion and a soft, high-pitched voice. She wore small glasses with frames that came to a point at the ends and wrapped her long, brown hair into a bun that crowned the top of her head. She dressed in long skirts that hung below her knees.

I remember Momma Hudson was a loving woman and always had handfuls of candy tucked inside her pockets, ready for distribution. We rarely had candy, so this was very special. She would place a few pieces into our little hands as a reward for learning scriptures or for helping with odd jobs around the orphanage.

Excitement bubbled up as Momma Hudson gave us the opportunity to memorize the books of the Bible. Those who recited them correctly would receive an award, and I was up for the challenge! She planned a picnic lunch on a beautiful beach with all of our favorites—vegetables, chicken, bread, and dessert— to cook right on the beach! She even purchased Champagne, a fruity-flavored soda, which was our favorite drink. I remember studying so hard, reciting the books over and over again, to make sure I could go. Finally, I stood in front of Momma Hudson, head held high with all the confidence in the world, and I did it. I remembered them all—a day on the beach was mine! It was a day of jubilation that I will never forget.

Being an adventurous man and curious about the battle ahead, Papa Hudson decided to attend several voodoo ceremonies. During one of them, a voodoo priest came up to him and said, "For fifty dollars I'll bring the devil out here and let you talk to him!"

"I don't want to talk to the devil," Papa Hudson replied coolly. "I've had too many fights with him!"

The priest stood in amazement and made a startling offer to the American. "For one hundred dollars," he declared, licking his lips, "I'll kill a man in front of you and drink his blood!"

Of course, Papa Hudson declined the sickening offer. But

now he knew what he was up against: pure evil.

Once the voodoo priest—called a houngan—heard about the church going up, he became very agitated. He didn't mind the orphanage, but a church was a threat to his temple. Every day he would march around the construction site wearing his brightly colored scarves, patched pants, and feathers, shaking his rattles, casting his spells, and proclaiming that anyone involved with the project would be cursed.

Papa and Momma Hudson continued the building project and believed the power of God that lived in them was greater than any devil.

We boys were always hanging around the building project trying to lend a helping hand. It actually was more getting in the way, but for us, being so close to the construction was too enticing. The loud sounds of the hammering caught my attention, and before long, I, too, was in the middle of the building venture. As I watched the men framing the roof and nailing boards into place, I could not resist the temptation to get a closer look. I slowly walked over and stood directly beneath the carpenters who were pounding away.

Within a split second, the hammer slipped from a carpenter's hand and crashed onto the top of my head, splitting it wide open. Blood streamed from the wound, running down my face and onto the ground. A loud scream rose from the pit of my stomach and echoed throughout the grounds. I grabbed my head and walked quickly toward Momma Hudson's apartment.

"Momma Hudson, Momma!" I cried. Within moments, she had me at the sink and was washing the wound, applying pressure, and using bandages to close the large gap. The wound left a scar that I have to this day as a reminder of my careless curiosity.

Finally, the construction project was complete. We were so excited! Concrete stairs lined the entrance to the bright white building. Bright, tropical flowers and a large, wooden podium stood on a wooden platform that stretched from wall to wall. Wooden benches sat in perfect rows down each side of the sanctuary.

Papa Hudson held a dedication service. The band played

jubilant melodies that welcomed guests as they filed into the beautiful new church. Women wore their best worn but neatly pressed dresses with white lace scarves covering their heads. Men wore button-up shirts neatly tucked into shabby dress pants and clutched tattered Bibles and handkerchiefs. Before entering the church, some of the men removed their shoes from underneath their arms, wiped them with a handkerchief, and put them on their feet. Many had walked for miles barefoot and only wore shoes in the house of Lord; they wanted to save their best for God.

Back at the orphanage, we boys were in our rooms rummaging through piles of clothing, searching for our best pieces. Shoes flew through the air, belts were fitted, and socks were paired up. We all wanted to look our best for the big dedication.

Finally we reached the church, filed through the door, marched up the center aisle, and sat down in the front rows. We felt proud and honored to have the support of the community; this church belonged to all of us.

The houngan heard the celebration from down the road and immediately marshaled his followers for an all-out confrontation. They danced up the road toward our church, the houngan leading the way blowing a long, slender horn. He was dressed in his circus-like attire as if he was some kind of Pied Piper.

Several people in the church heard the houngan coming and informed the Hudsons. "They're going to circle the church and put a spell on it!" they exclaimed.

"They're not going around this church!" Momma Hudson declared. The band stopped playing as she marched out the door to meet the uninvited evildoers. The houngan's horn kept blaring as he marched up the steps to where Momma Hudson stood. He began to march his followers around the building when Momma Hudson jumped out in front of him. The houngan blared his horn at her, and he and his group began a lewd dance filled with vulgar gestures.

"You really think you're something. I'll just look you right in the eye until you get enough of it and leave!" Momma Hudson spoke with boldness. She didn't care that he didn't understand English. He could tell that whatever she was saying, she meant it.

This was a situation the houngan didn't know how to handle: a little white woman blocking his way. Papa Hudson quickly joined his wife. With the two of them standing in his way, the priest finally turned and walked off with the other worshippers following him.

It was a big night. Four hundred people worshipped exuberantly, clapping, dancing, and raising their hands toward the sky. They shouted prayers for our orphanage, our church, and our island. Papa Van's son Rick preached with vigor.

As the service neared its end, an invitation to receive the Lord was given. A young man came forward and kneeled at the altar. He was visibly touched—tears poured from his face. Rick leaned over, laid his hands on the man's head, and began to pray with authority. The man surrendered his life to the Lord.

A big stir arose in the audience. People were pointing and speaking outwardly. "He's the houngan's son!" they shouted.

This was a miraculous sign to everyone that the power of God was greater than all the teaching the boy had received from his father. Papa's dream was fulfilled, and God soon drove out the evil powers that had lurked outside our gate.

Just In Time

The day was in full force. I had walked down the lush, green path, shuffling my feet through the overgrown grass that led to an outhouse. Sweat ran down my face and dripped off my chin as the unbearable heat blanketed the island.

Blood poured down from the rock and onto the ground where I had been kneeling for some time, trying to relieve the discomfort. Something was wrong; once again, I was afflicted by a bleeding tumor. This one had formed inside my large intestine and prevented me from properly eliminating waste from my body. I felt unbearable pressure from the inside out, and relief came only from the release of blood.

As I leaned against a tree in an effort to regain my energy, I glanced up and met the eyes of an uninvited spectator—another boy who lived at the orphanage. He watched as blood trickled around my feet, soaking the ground.

My secret was exposed! I was mortified. I hadn't told a single soul about what was happening. How could I explain such a private problem? How could I share this without being made fun of? But now it was out and, in some ways, I felt a little relieved. I also was comforted when I learned the other boy had only told the orphanage director, who questioned me and then went to work getting word to Papa Van. Now that Papa knew, I was sure it would only be a matter of time before he would send help.

Just as I thought, it only took about a month before Papa came. The sun beat down and reflected heat off the tin roof. It was a workday, and we were busy cleaning up the grounds. Some of the boys washed walls while others cleaned off walkways and picked up garbage that was scattered around our fifteen acres.

Sweat poured off my face, and my body became weak and unstable as I struggled to keep up with my tasks. My heart raced, and I gasped to catch my breath. The sounds of the boys became muffled, and the light of the day tunneled into darkness. I tumbled onto the ground, flat on my back, out and unresponsive.

I found myself in this predicament over and over again. I wanted to play and run with the other boys, but often my physical condition forced me to sit on the sidelines. Momma and Papa Hudson kept a watchful eye on me. Not fully understanding the cause of my symptoms, they sought the limited medical treatment that Haiti offered. For more than a year, I fought fatigue, experienced lightheadedness, and had blackouts. Pure exhaustion ruled my days, rendering me useless and needing extra sleep.

Did God bring me back to Haiti to die? I had been through a lot in my ten years of life. I had already learned to trust God; with so many changes, He had been my only constant. I knew my miracle would come. And it did—just in the nick of time.

"Papa! Papa!" The boys' shouts echoed through the property. My papa was here! He had taught me so much, but the greatest was to trust God. If anyone was going to get me through this medical crisis, it would be Papa Van.

I jumped to my feet, overwhelmed with the excitement of Papa Van's arrival. I grabbed my drum and stood on the orphanage steps waiting for him and his guests. As soon as Papa was in position, we started our grand welcoming celebration with our horns, drums, guitars, and singing.

Our band's audience was an American medical team. Each member stood at the bottom of the stairs beaming up at us. At my lowest point of medical despair, each smiling face represented my miracle.

As the colors of dawn spread across the sky the next morning, this outstanding team of American medical professionals was ready to serve us with the donated medical equipment they'd brought. At this early hour, a line of boys already trailed down the stairs of the orphanage to the large trucks that were loaded to capacity. The excitement was almost tangible as boys and medical missionaries carried dental chairs, medical equipment, and supplies inside.

We had picked out a room off the main entrance to serve as our new health center. We could hardly contain our enthusiasm as we washed the walls and swept the concrete floors with rags and buckets of soapy water. We rejoiced as we lined the room with rows of the new medical equipment.

We quickly named this space *The Clinic* and wasted no time in forming a line. It was exciting to watch the medical experts work their magic as we each waited for our turn. They cleaned our teeth, checked our blood pressure, and performed other medical procedures.

After waiting and watching the others, my heart began to pound with anticipation. In many ways I felt relief that my "medical secret" had been revealed. I knew I needed help, and now was not the time to let pride and embarrassment keep me from the aid I so desperately needed. The medical team thoroughly examined my face—sticking their hands in my mouth, pushing, pulling, and rubbing. They found three more tumors: one on the left side of my jaw, another on my right cheek, and the third in the right section of my neck. These tumors were visible, but they were nothing compared to the bleeding tumor in my lower large intestine. It had weakened me considerably, and once again, I found myself hanging in the balance. Without proper medical care, I would die.

With his unfailing determination, Papa Van arranged for my lifesaving procedures. A couple of months later I found myself in a familiar place: thirty thousand feet above the blue-green waters of the Caribbean, soaring through the clouds, returning to America to receive another medical miracle.

The frogs and crickets began their early evening songs as we rounded a corner in Jacksonville, Florida. The sun, nearly sunk below the horizon, gave one final display of rich, red hues. Enthusiasm bubbled up from within me as we drove through the crowded streets. It had been a long day of changing planes and navigating airports. Papa Van was unable to accompany me on this trip, but since I was eleven years old and had the assistance of a friendly flight attendant, I was able to make the journey on my own. I had finally arrived, and this peaceful drive through the coastal city was welcoming. Around each corner was a delightful discovery of small beach shops and seaside cafes.

As I took in the new sights, I glanced over at the driver—a kind, soft-spoken man named Dr. Schellhase. He was the dentist who had examined me several months earlier in Haiti, so I was familiar with him. Papa knew him well and was confident enough to let me venture alone to Jacksonville.

As we weaved in and out of traffic, I couldn't help but wonder about my medical happenstance. It seemed to overwhelm my existence, and the urgency of it had brought me far from home to another unfamiliar city. Thankfully, Dr. Schellhase was able to reassure me and calm my jitters.

By now, the bright red hues from the sunset had diffused into the softness of twilight. The warm sea-salt air blew through the car as we slowly maneuvered over several speed bumps. With one final bounce and a slight turn, we reached our first destination.

Large palm trees, tropical blooms lined the way to large glass door at the entrance of the dentist's office. Inside, a waiting room was filled with fabric chairs, end tables, and patients reading magazines while waiting for their appointments. To help pass time, Dr. Schellhase led me into a private room and offered me a drink and a snack. Within moments of my arrival, the small room buzzed with delightful people, welcoming hugs, and warm smiles. I already knew the beautiful dental assistants, as they had been part of Dr. Schellhase's medical team in Haiti.

I broke into a big smile when I caught a glimpse of her bright smile peeking in from behind the door. Debbie, one of Dr. Schellhase's assistants, scurried through the room and wrapped her arms tightly around my shoulders, giving me the biggest heartfelt hug. Papa Van had arranged for me to stay with her and her husband, Arthur, a surgeon. I will never forget them. They were young, energetic, and hard workers. They had no children, so the task of caring for me was one they welcomed.

Clean, pristine homes with grand entryways, flowery walking paths and manicured lawns lined the freshly paved streets in Arthur and Debbie's upscale neighborhood, and couples walked hand-in-hand along the smooth sidewalks. This was too much to believe! How could I so quickly go from rags to riches? Again, I found myself going from Haiti to hope. My eyes widened in disbelief as we slowly maneuvered into the drive. Could this be their house—and my new temporary home?

As we walked through the main entry, I stretched my neck upward to peer at the large vaulted ceilings. A beautiful kitchen opened up to a grand family room. Off to one side, big, beautiful columns separated it from a spacious dining room.

Within moments, a loud, deep rumbling echoed throughout the house. Suddenly the biggest, fluffiest dog I had ever seen flew around the corner, sliding on the tile with his big furry paws leading the way. He almost knocked me to the ground as his big, slobbery tongue covered my face, leaving behind a sticky slime. My heart nearly pounded out of my chest! This massive, brown and white St. Bernard ruled this space, and with a few more welcoming licks, he accepted me into the family.

A room down the hallway had been prepared for me. Sitting against one wall was a large wooden bed with oversized blankets and pillows. A matching dresser with a mirror flanked the opposite wall. Everything was new and appeared to be custom-made, ordered just for my arrival.

I settled in quickly, and before long we were in the routine of weekday work schedules, weekend trips to the park, and family dinners. I loved my new home and family.

A few weeks and several medical examinations later, it was determined that I was too young to undergo such an intricate surgery; I would need to wait at least a year before I could have the operations I needed. Oh my goodness! I was thrilled to be able to wait in this beautiful American home.

Every night Arthur would tuck me into bed, read me a story, and kiss my forehead. I felt so loved. Calling Arthur and Debbie "Dad" and "Mom" came easily.

Even though I knew it was a temporary situation, I prayed that it would somehow become permanent. Every child deserves a permanent place to call home, and this seemed like the perfect place for me.

I still thought of Momma and Dad in Haiti. I loved them so much, but I knew that in Haiti the orphanage would always be my home. My parents were barely surviving themselves, making it impossible for them to care for me.

For the last several years I had felt like a ship without a sail, blowing in the wind at the mercy of the sea, my emotions tossed to and fro. Now, even if for a short time, I had an anchor that came in the form of two wonderful people who had no connections to Haiti—two magnificent people I now called Mom and Dad.

My life was good—no, it was spectacular. I felt like a carefree child with no worries or responsibilities. I spent my days with the little fireball who lived two doors down—a girl with short, brown hair and big brown eyes who was tougher than any boy I had ever known.

Our imaginations carried us to far-away lands where we would fight the bad guys and rule kingdoms. In our play, the neighborhood transformed into a world of castles, fair maidens, and brave knights. On hot summer days, pirates would come ashore and chase us down, looking for lost treasure. We would balance ourselves just right, carefully boosting ourselves off the curb and onto our oversized bicycles. We rode them like rockets, darting through the neighborhood, down wooded paths, and to the candy store. Our pockets loaded with tasty treats, we would zoom back down the paths, laughing as if we had landed the pirates' treasure.

Playing with this girl became medicine to my soul. The burden of my Haitian family and the hardship of their lives became a distant memory entangled within the fantasy of play. For brief moments in time, reality could be whatever we wanted it to be. We were two friends creating our own world of the spectacular—a world of friendship and pleasant childhood memories.

I wanted this dream of an all-American family to last forever, but it was cut short abruptly. I made a mistake—one serious misstep that brought my dream to a sudden halt.

Arthur and Debbie worked hard during the week and looked forward to spending the weekends together, often leaving me home alone. One particular night, feeling a little fearful, I did the unthinkable: I lied. I called them and told them that I was bleeding—which for me meant life-threatening hemorrhaging. They hurried home, expecting a serious medical disaster, only to find me snuggled up on the couch fast asleep, my arms wrapped around the fluffy St. Bernard. I was perfectly fine, just scared and lonely. Talk about regret. Within moments, my American family slipped away beyond my reach.

After only nine months of living the American dream, I found myself reluctantly leaving a place of hope and returning to a place of despair. I was traveling back to Haiti—a place I knew all too well—where I would finish out the waiting until I could withstand my next surgery.

The heat was like a smoldering blanket hanging overhead as large raindrops splattered in mud puddles. Boys wearing little to nothing waited patiently as they danced around, forming a line. Liquid soap bubbled up through the air as Momma Van poured a generous amount onto the concrete ramp, and without hesitation, the slip-and-slide was in full force. Fifty boys went flying down the ramp like sudsy rockets, one right after the other, twisting and turning, gliding down on their tummies, backs, and bottoms. A sea of white, soapy foam and a quick-thinking Momma Van made for a delightful afternoon.

I had been back in Haiti for almost a year and was thrilled to have Momma and Papa Van visiting. They loved me unconditionally, and their constant presence brought me a sense of stability. Even though they had many children to tend to, I always felt special. I believed Momma Van favored me over the others. Although she was careful to be fair to all the boys, I could tell that I was her favorite by the way she would sneak money or special treats into my pocket.

After receiving these special blessings from Momma Van, I would travel home to Carrefour with my older brother Jean to share these riches with my struggling family. Momma Van would also send for my younger sisters to give them dresses, sandals, and little girl treasures she had set aside just for them—things they could have never had otherwise. It was always wonderful to see my family and even more wonderful to see the smiles on their faces. We always had a great weekend together. Momma Van made sure I had enough money for taptap fare and food, along with leftovers to share, so that I could be a blessing.

I loved being able to travel home to spend time with my family. They were the poorest of the poor—they had no beds, tables, or chairs, no electricity or indoor plumbing, and they often went without food. They wore rags and went barefoot. The struggle to survive was overwhelming, but in the midst of the desolation, they found peace. It came bubbling up from within each one of them. They found joy in the simplest of things. They loved life, and they loved each other. Happiness didn't come from what they did or didn't have, but true joy flowed from the inside out, transforming our makeshift hut into a loving home. They had value simply because they existed—value that went beyond opinions, material goods, or preconceived notions. They were priceless. They were my family, and I loved them.

We laughed, played games, and listened to Dad as he retold old Haitian tales. The open cooking fire reduced to ash. Smoke still billowed through the air, leaving the distinct smell of burnt embers. The sun, casting its radiant glow of yellow and orange, sank beneath the hills. Dad, who was wearing a worn-out button-up shirt with missing buttons and cut-off pants, sat in the dirt with his back against the outside wall of our hut. His knees were bent, his bare feet resting in the ashy-dirt mixture surrounding the home. I walked over to him and watched as he nodded off to sleep. I dipped my fingertips into the ash below, then gently grabbed a strand of his grey hair, paused briefly, and pulled it from his head. Dad opened his eyes and grinned. I took another grey strand and pulled, repeating the pattern. Dad closed his eyes. He loved this relaxing grooming, and within moments, he was fast asleep.

Time went by too quickly, and soon it was time to say

goodbye, which was never easy. It was especially hard for my mom, not knowing when she would see me next. I felt I was big; after all, I was twelve years old and had lived away from home for seven years. But that didn't matter to Momma; I was her baby, and saying goodbye was heartbreaking.

Big tears filled her eyes as she wrapped her thin arms around my shoulders. She paused for a moment, rocking me back and forth, almost as if I were the five-year-old child she had let go so many years earlier. Once again, those familiar questions must have bombarded her mind. Will he get the help he needs? Will he make it through the surgery? Will I see him again?

We had said goodbye many times before, but most times I was going back to the orphanage after a weekend reunion. This time was different. Instead of returning to the orphanage, I would be leaving my homeland once again to receive another life saving surgery.

I felt torn between wanting to be with my family and wanting to be free of the hardship to which life in Haiti had enslaved us. The burden of breaking my family's captivity to poverty pressed in on me, resting upon my shoulders. For Momma, this goodbye was much more than my leaving for another surgery—it was hope for a better future. She wanted freedom from poverty, but more so, she wanted her son to be free, even if it meant saying goodbye.

The sweltering sun was already breaking over the horizon as I boarded the giant aircraft with Papa and Momma Van. It was mid-morning, and we would not be arriving in Evansville until sundown.

Papa had made the arrangements for my next surgery, and it could not have come soon enough. I was in dire need of medical intervention. Over the past several years, my battle with blood loss, blackouts, and physical deficiencies had taken its toll, and I found myself getting tired doing the simplest tasks. I was relieved to be back in America. The conveniences of air conditioning, proper bathroom facilities, and better nutrition helped make this medical hardship a little easier to bear.

After spending a few weeks in Evansville, Papa Van and I

were off on our next adventure. My wait was finally over! At last, now being thirteen, I was old enough to withstand the intricate surgery. Everything was in order, and we were making our way to Gainesville, Florida.

Papa thought driving his motorhome would be the best option for this road trip. Momma Van had stocked it with food, utensils, bedding, and special treats. Papa always had to have his sweets: Twinkies, peanut M&M's, and Hostess cupcakes, which he hid in dresser drawers, cabinets, and bedside stands. He often even kept several tasty delights in his pockets and pop them into his mouth as we traveled down the road. When his pockets were empty, I rummaged around looking for more.

We drove down the highway telling stories, acting silly, and listening to music. I remember Papa putting in the Sons of Faith cassette tape. Papa's son Rick was a singer in the group, and this was their new recording. We drove down the highway singing, our mouths full of Hostess cakes and peanuts. I'm surprised we didn't choke!

I'm sure Papa had a multitude of important tasks to do, but he never made me feel like a burden or a second-class citizen. He made me feel important.

As we journeyed down the road with the windows open and music blaring, I realized that this man loved me like a son. I had long searched for a place to belong, and even though I was still an orphan, I had Papa. He had given me wonderful memories and imprinted my heart with the love of a father.

Before long, we arrived at our temporary destination: Gainesville Teaching Hospital. The medical community poured out its love once again, donating everything needed to save my life.

The men and women of Bible Center Cathedral also chipped in to help with travel expenses. Their constant giving to Haiti Christian Orphanage brought me out of absolute medical despair and into a place of hope.

Since morning would bring with it a gamut of medical testing, Papa and I settled in early for the night. The moon was shining bright, casting its soft glow through the window blinds of the RV. The night was quiet and peaceful. As I lay there trying to calm my nerves and rest my eyes, the aroma of chocolate filled the air. With one sniff and a peek through the darkness, it dawned on me that Papa was enjoying a tasty treat.

"Goodnight, Papa," I said.

"Goodnight," Papa replied, his mouth full of chocolate.

At sunrise, Papa and I made our way into the hospital. I was used to hospitals now, so it didn't take long to get into my gown, hop into bed, and turn on the television. I knew this would be a waiting game, and I couldn't think of a better way to pass the time than watching a few good shows. *Emergency* was my favorite program. With my strong Haitian accent, I would beg, "Please Papa, let's watch e-mercy. Let's watch e-mercy." I had to repeat myself several times before Papa could make sense of what I was saying. By the time I finished the first episode, nurses were ready to wheel me down the hall to another room.

The next several days were filled with one test after another. It was a whirlwind of procedures—scans, x-rays, blood draws, and dye pumped through my arteries. The medical staff put me into and onto different machines that rotated my body every which way. I felt like a medical mystery on display.

Since this was a teaching hospital, I became a living textbook for more than a hundred eager medical students. Any dignity or personal privacy I may have had went right out the window. Students observed with clipboards in hand while a medical doctor poked, probed, and explained my medical details.

Because of the medical tests, I was not allowed to eat. What I would have given for one of Papa's tasty snacks! In Haiti I had gone without food many times, but after Papa's road trip of food overload, I was feeling deprived. As hungry as I felt and as unpleasant as this was, though, I was still relieved this day had come. I was finally going to be delivered from the life-draining tumors.

Late into the evening of the second day, it was determined that I needed several blood transfusions. The medical professionals couldn't believe I was doing so well, given the large tumor embedded in my colon and the frequent loss of blood. I also had severe anemia, which could lead to heart failure. It was a miracle I was still alive. Blood was brought in throughout the night to replenish what I had lost, and the medical staff spent several days stabilizing me in preparation for the surgeries.

Countless doctors, nurses, medical students, and machines surrounded my bed, but within seconds of arriving in the operating room, I was out in a drug-induced slumber. I don't know how many hours my operations lasted, but the surgeons started when the sun rose and finished after it set.

Surgeons worked for hours to remove a hemangioma from the left portion of my jaw, another from the right side of my neck, and a third from the right side of my cheek. The blood vessels relaxed during the surgery, complicating their removal. The surgeons had trouble distinguishing the clear boundary of where the hemangiomas started and ended, resulting in only a partial removal. They made a four-inch incision to remove the tumor on my neck and another incision on the left side of my jaw to remove the one in my cheek. To minimize scarring, another three-inch incision was made inside my mouth to remove the tumor along my jaw. After many attempts to completely remove the hemangiomas, it was decided to leave the remnants of abnormal tissue, as they would not be life threatening. A drainage tube was left in my jaw to assist with the healing process.

After completing the procedures on my jaw and neck, the surgeons went on to remove the hemangioma that was buried within my colon. The tangled mass of blood vessels had grown into a large tumor that protruded down, causing blockage and blood loss. This tumor was rare, so the medical students were jumping at the opportunity to witness such an enlightening procedure. After many hours, removal was complete.

It was a success! The troublesome tumors would no longer hold me captive. God's miracles had no shortage, and I was still alive because of His unfailing love.

Childhood Adventures

After several weeks in the hospital, I was finally released. Papa Van and I traveled back to Evansville, Indiana, where I continued my recovery. Several doctors in the Evansville area had graciously taken over my medical care, removing the drainage tubes. I was on the mend.

Staying with Momma and Papa Van while I recovered was a blessing. Momma Van had prepared a room for me in the basement of their cozy home. She covered the bed with a pink silk bedspread, placed a small lamp on a bedside stand, and stood a dresser against the wall. Pink wouldn't have been my first choice, but Momma Van loved it, so that was the color scheme of my new home away from home. With everything they had done for me, though, enduring the color wasn't so difficult. To add to the delightful décor, Momma laid a black Raggedy Andy doll on my bed. I appreciated her efforts and was thrilled to have the blessings this luxurious home offered.

Staying with Momma and Papa Van was quite entertaining. Papa could hardly hear, and Momma could barely see. Each evening at five o'clock, while Momma was rushing around in the kitchen making dinner, Papa and I would relax on the couch in the living room. I watched television and played with Bobi, and Papa glanced through the newspaper, holding it up to that it covered his entire face. Momma jabbered her demands at him as she pranced around and he read, complaining in frustration about being ignored after repeating herself several times. Without missing a beat, Papa lowered his paper, winked at me, and made the crazy sign, mouthing the word "cuckoo." He had heard everything she said. I just grinned and kept silent. His secret was safe with me and convenient for him.

In the evenings, Momma Van and I would go into her room to watch television. She would sit on her bed, gently resting her head against the headboard, while I sat near the end of the bed. I would prop her tired feet onto a pile of pillows, pour some lotion on my hands, and begin the nightly routine of rubbing her feet. We would sit for an hour or two watching our favorite cowboy flick. She enjoyed cowboy pictures just as much as I did, and I loved spending evenings with Momma. Even though she thought she got the better end of the deal with a nightly foot massage, I was the real winner.

Momma Van would often yell for Papa: "Alf, Alf, Alf!" When he did not respond, she would squint her eyes and stick out her tongue. I would get so tickled and laugh out loud. Through our laughter, she would yell louder. When Papa still would not respond, she again squinted her eyes, stuck out her tongue and blew out just enough to make a funny noise. I loved every second and laughed harder and louder.

Momma Van loved snacks almost as much as Papa. Late into the evening, she would often decide suddenly, "Let's get some hot rice with milk and sugar." I didn't complain—it was one of my favorites, and I loved midnight munchies. We would march back to her room with our arms full of drinks and treats, and then settle in for another Wild West adventure.

There was never a dull moment. Momma and Papa Van found happiness in the simple things of life. They enjoyed just being together and turning an ordinary evening into a lifetime of special memories.

Julie

"I know you're down there!" her high-pitched voice echoed down the stairs. There was no use trying to hide from her; I knew she would find me. Soon enough, she came running down the basement stairs, her blonde pigtails bouncing. She gazed up at me with her big blue eyes as she flashed a bright smile, seemingly carefree as she pranced around the room with her bigger-than-life personality.

She was Papa's granddaughter, Julie. She loved spending time at Papa's house and with me. But I was thirteen years old, and spending the day with an energetic four-year-old girl was not high on my priority list.

Soon after her arrival, Momma Van yelled down the stairs, "Reeser, you play with that baby! She came all the way here to see you!"

Julie quickly gathered up baby dolls, stuffed animals, and books and placed them in neat rows. She stood up on the bed, a book in hand, and recited her salvation message. She pointed her finger, sang her song, and raised her voice until she felt content with our repentance. Then she climbed off the bed and onto my lap.

Julie insisted on having my full attention all afternoon. She gave me baby dolls to dress and Barbie dolls to fix. She rambled on about her make-believe world, not letting me get a word in edgewise; she talked from the moment she arrived until the moment she left. She climbed up onto my shoulders, hanging on with her hands wrapped around my neck, laughing and giggling as she climbed down my waist and slid around my legs onto the floor. She jumped up and down, giggling as if she had conquered Mt. Everest. "Doesn't she ever slow down or get tired? Isn't it her naptime?" I wondered.

Julie coerced me with that bright smile to sit and watch while she performed songs, dance routines, and tumbling acts. At least I enjoyed that more than the climbing routine she had performed on me earlier. I was happy to sit for a moment—being a spectator was much easier than being a battered participant! I clapped after each performance, watching as she threw her hands to the sky, bent her knees, and gave a most impressive curtsy.

After a short pause, she skipped over to where I was sitting and suggested that the next routine deserved a grand introduction. So I raised my voice and made the announcement: "Ladies and gentlemen, for your entertainment—the one, the only, Julie." Darting from the corner to the middle of the room, Julie was ready for her moment in the spotlight. I must have watched more than a hundred performances.

"Julie! Julie!" Momma Van finally hollered from the top of the stairs. Those were the best words I could have heard. She was going home, and I could finally rest. After one final bounce onto my back and a kiss goodbye, she scurried up the stairs for her grand exit.

I cleaned up some dolls, threw my exhausted body onto my bed, let out a huge sigh, and thanked God I had survived. At last, I had peace and quiet.

It was 1978. After staying two years with Papa and Momma Van, my medical visa was about to expire. I was a little older now, and with the pressing need to return to Haiti, Papa had concerns about my ability to provide a living for myself. I would be returning to the orphanage, but within a few years I would have to leave and face the unknown outside the orphanage gates.

In Haiti, more than 60 percent of the population is unemployed.[iv] Due to the lack of provision, many families expect that children will join the work force at age fifteen.

Papa, being resourceful and thoughtful, had the perfect solution: he would teach me a trade. I was going to be a locksmith! He had been given key-making machinery and supplies so that I would be well equipped and prepared for a successful future.

I held up the large red textbook, *Everything You Need to Know About Becoming a Locksmith*, which covered half of my body and felt like it weighed a ton. It had hundreds of pages—all written in English.

Papa would often ask, "Reeser, have you studied your book?"

"Yes, Papa," I would reply. It was important to Papa that I learn a trade and secure a future in the midst of uncertainty. Papa knew I was a survivor, and with a little help, I would have an advantage.

Papa wanted all the boys in the orphanage to learn a vocation. He sent machinery to Haiti in hopes that we would become skillful craftsmen, because he knew that this would be our best chance for survival outside the orphanage.

I tried to learn the art of key making but quickly lost interest. Although I didn't learn the trade, the life lessons Papa taught me penetrated deep within my soul.

Papa wanted to make a difference, and he did, one child at a time. He invested his emotions, time, money, and love. I would soon be returning to Haiti, but the investment Papa had made into my life would be with me forever. Regardless of where I lived, his awe-inspiring example would remain.

The years I lived with Momma and Papa Van transformed my existence. By watching and listening to Papa, I learned that God does not give you what you can handle, but He helps you handle what you have been given. I learned that family is having someone to love. Momma and Papa Van, the boys at the orphanage, and my mom and dad—I loved them all, and they were my family. I learned that a home is having a place to lay your head. Whether it was on the dirt floor of a mud hut, in a cozy bed with comfy pillows, or on a straw mattress at the orphanage, I had a home. And most of all, I learned that I was lucky enough to have both a family and a home, and that made me blessed.

The familiar scent of coals burning from the open fires of my homeland billowed through the air, flooding my mind with precious memories of my mom's meals. The dusty film lay overhead as cars, taptaps, and hundreds of pedestrians filled the sidewalks and surrounding streets. I followed closely behind Momma and Papa Van as we made our way through the hustle and bustle. Men were speaking loudly in Creole, fighting with one another as they grabbed at Papa's luggage. Each man was pulling and fussing in hopes that he would receive a tip—desperately needed money to survive another day. Even though Momma was used to Haitian drama, I stuck close to her side.

I felt proud to be back in Haiti. Momma Van had bought me a new cowboy outfit, which I wore with pride. I was the best-looking Haitian cowboy anyone had ever seen—or maybe the *only* Haitian cowboy anyone had ever seen. I wore the toughest, roughest cowboy pants ever made, a two-tone brown and white satin shirt with classic cowboy embroidery, cowboy-tough boots made from the finest leather money could buy, and the best part of the whole ensemble—my cowboy hat. Oh, yes, Momma had picked out the John Wayne cowboy look-alike hat. I was cowboy-ready from head to toe, and I felt like a famous American cowboy who had stepped right out of a movie and into a tropical mishap.

Several small children under the age of ten, wearing nothing more than rags, had made their way to Momma Van. They were barefoot, filthy, and exuded a very unpleasant odor. You could tell by their appearance that they were street kids—abandoned and left to fend for themselves. Momma secretly slipped each of them a dollar bill. She was careful to not let anyone see, since it's against Haitian law to beg; it also is very dangerous. Children have lost their lives for less than a few dollars. Unfortunately, due to extreme poverty, life has little value, and the threat of losing it for a few dollars is a real concern.

After shuffling through the sea of chaos, we got into a rental car and began our careful journey through the crowded streets that led to the orphanage. Excitement rose up inside of me as I thought about seeing the boys at the orphanage and my family in Carrefour.

I wondered if this would be my last adventure leading to my final home. As we drove closer to the orphanage, the wonderful realization of my two very different worlds came over me. I felt blessed to have had the opportunity to experience both: one full of opportunity and abundance, the other overwhelmed with hardship and the struggle to survive. Each location had its own place in carving my character and shaping the person I had become. I was the lucky one in a world so vast and rich with experiences. I had the opportunity to venture out into the unknown and live.

The orphanage was always full of activity and childhood adventures. It didn't take long, and like a red rocket, I sped down the mountainous hill on our new toy—a moped that Momma and Papa Van had purchased in America while I was living with them.

The engine blared as I accelerated full speed ahead. A cloud of smoke filled the air, leaving the smell of hot motor oil. Fifty boys followed behind, running as fast as they could, trying to keep up and grabbing onto the sides of the roaring motorbike. They had never seen anything so marvelous.

When we reached the bottom of the hill, the boys stood in awe. Most were speechless as they ran their hands over the chrome fenders, bright red paint, and shiny handlebars. Standing in disbelief, they began to clap and rejoice with excitement.

One after the other, each boy took a turn zooming down the hill. It was the greatest entertainment the orphanage had ever seen. Every day for months, from sun up to sun down, we would ride as if we were members of a drag racing team. Even though this machine was only a moped, in our minds it was a high-speed racing bike. We showed no mercy! We would fly down the hill, hitting boulders, potholes, and trees, and laughing at each other as our bodies flew over the handlebars and landed on the hard ground. Three boys at a time would push the bike beyond its capacity, holding on tightly as they sped out of control down the mountainous terrain. A dust cloud engulfed the hillside as we shouted, laughed, and celebrated the greatest invention we had ever laid our hands on. We would return to the orphanage with bloody knees and elbows, dirty faces, and grease-stained clothes.

That moped was the highlight of our days. But not surprisingly, it wasn't long before it was reduced to a pile of broken metal. One bike for more than fifty boys—it was certainly well used and enjoyed. While it lasted, it had transformed the back property into a world of motocross and fast-paced adventure.

Since we had developed a need for speed, we had no choice but to be innovative after the sad demise of our moped. Our resources were limited, so we were used to making something from nothing. We transformed sticks into boats; rocks became marbles; discarded garbage became game pieces. But now that we had tasted the reckless thrill of speed, we had moved beyond child's play. Suddenly, discarded garbage and stick boats were for little boys.

At least a dozen boys followed behind as I dragged a large round barrel up the hill. We had worn a wide dirt path where we raced our moped, and this would be the perfect spot for our next reckless venture. I positioned the barrel at the top of the hill and centered it with the roughly worn path.

Without hesitation, I jumped inside the barrel. It spiraled down the path, bouncing over boulders, rolling through patches of grass, and careening into trees, shaking me from one end to the other. My arms flailed about as my legs pressed hard against the sides, trying to stay inside. It seemed to pick up speed like an uncontrolled missile. Round and round I plummeted, and my exhilarated laughter echoed throughout the countryside.

The other boys ran down the hill kicking up a thick trail of dust. Once the barrel reached the bottom, I remained inside for a moment to overcome my dizziness. When the boys reached the bottom of the hill, they yelled and pounded on the top of the barrel, thrilled and excited about our newfound rollercoaster adventure. After regaining my composure, I crawled out, jumped to my feet, and gave victorious high-fives. We had conquered our need for speed.

We grabbed the barrel and quickly ran back up the hill. As the boys waited for their turns, organized chaos took over the hillside. The racing barrel became like a high-paced amusement park ride. Making something out of nothing was what we did best, and this makeshift ride was the best thing we had ever created.

At the orphanage, we had fun and created adventure out of everyday life. It did not matter that we would never visit spectacular places or have the childhood inventions we dreamed about. Instead, it was about who was beside us as we ventured through our day-to-day lives. Having each other filled our hearts and turned our impoverished orphanage into a world of cherished childhood memories.

The sun was setting, casting an orange-red glow, leaving just enough light to still see. The walls around our beds reflected the crimson light as we prepared our room for the night, quickly organized our belongings before total darkness set in. Since we didn't have electricity, we had learned the importance of getting things done while daylight remained.

As night approached, I snuggled onto my straw mattress, trying to find a comfortable position. I was now fourteen years old and had much more experience with fixing the holes and bending the straw that had poked through the thin material over time. Although I was a little restless, I eventually surrendered to the exhaustion brought on by our barrel racing adventure.

The sticky heat saturated our room, causing sweat to pour down our tired bodies. Even though I was miserably hot, I could not help but cover my face in fear when I heard the voodoo drums pounding in the distance. My mind raced with thoughts of the evil acts being performed under the darkness of night by the voodoo priest. Covering my face also helped keep the mosquitoes at bay. I prayed that a small breeze would blow and give us some relief from the smoldering heat. If only I could muster up a bit of courage, just enough to uncover my face, it would relieve some of the unbearable discomfort. I couldn't decide what I hated most: the heat, the mosquitoes, or the voodoo drums.

Nighttime seemed to bring many troublesome distractions, like the rats we heard scurrying above us on the tin roof as they searched for garbage. We had become accustomed to their meddling and could easily ignore their curious scampering, but one distraction was too difficult to ignore: bed bugs! These pesky insects had made themselves at home, feasting on us throughout the night and leading to restless nights and itchy days. Hovering between a sleepy slumber and a painful reality, we would scoop up the bugs in our hands and smash them against the concrete wall. Eventually, our extermination method left bloody stripes along the white walls.

We could survive the rats, the unbearable heat, the voodoo drums, and the uncomfortable mattresses, but bed bugs…oh Lord, why bugs?

As the sun peeked over the horizon, we gathered on the front stairs of the orphanage to plot what I called "Operation Take Down." Since none of us had experience with such a significant task, we thought it best to strategize.

We could hear the pig grunting as he uprooted some shrubs alongside of the building. Papa and Momma had bought the strong, stout hog for us to raise. We heard the quick, hard thumping of his hooves as we plotted our plan. Within moments, it was decided: the pig would be sacrificed to make provision for our historic Christmas dinner. We rarely got to eat meat, so this was a big deal.

Predictably, with more than fifty boys involved, our plan quickly turned into childhood chaos. Desire to conquer the beast rose up in each one of us, but catching the pig was more challenging than we expected. The fifteen acres of property suddenly became a hunting ground. He was out there somewhere, and we were determined to find him.

We began running and zigzagging through the bushes and down the dusty, rocky terrain. The pig took off like an out-of-control firecracker. Dust went flying as we battled with the uncontrollable beast. Up the hill we flew, and down the hill we tumbled. We tried jumping on his back and grabbing at his feet, but his rough hide would slip beyond our reach. The pig squealed and contorted his porky body. Round and round we ran. We were yelling; the pig was screaming. Finally, in the crazy frenzy, "Operation Take Down" became a success.

We had destroyed the orphanage landscape in the process of our "take down," but the reward of filling our bellies with tasty pork was worth it. Our overseer began meticulously cutting the meat into large portions, preparing it for our Christmas celebration. Nothing would be wasted; meat was such a rarity. Every part of the animal would be prepared for food—even the blood would be made into a tasty blood sausage.

We were excited about Christmas dinner, but it was still a few days away. We were hungry now, and after the exhausting hunt, we were famished and ready for a taste. We gathered around the carcass and cut off small sections of pork.

The sun was starting to set and we felt the urgency to prepare our treats before sundown. We scattered throughout the grounds, each one of us carrying a small portion of meat. Our mouths watered with the thought of sinking our teeth into the tasty morsels. I had been blessed with eating meat in America, but this was a momentous occasion for the other boys at the orphanage, and they could hardly contain their excitement.

I wandered around until I found the perfect spot. I carefully rummaged through the garbage for an aluminum can, which I transformed into a makeshift cooking pot. I gathered up some dry branches, tossed them into a pile, and set them ablaze. I patiently waited until it burned down into rich, red embers, making it perfect for cooking.

As the sun set over the hill, the landscape glowed with bright flames flickering back and forth through the darkness. The bright dancing lights grew as each boy cooked on his own makeshift outdoor stove. The whispering hisses, sizzling pops, and a thick, intoxicating smell of musky smoke and roasting pork filled the air.

The savory, tender meat melted in my mouth. Pure satisfaction! In the stillness of the night, with our tummies full and the black sky abounding with bright stars, we quietly appreciated the blessing. "Operation Take Down" was a success, and we had just begun to enjoy its rewards.

Sunbeams danced through the partially screened windows, lighting up the room where we bunked as a rooster cried his early morning melody. The room buzzed with anticipation; it was our favorite time of year! Papa and Momma Van would be arriving at the orphanage today to celebrate Christmas with us, and we could hardly contain our excitement as we jumped from bed to bed, chanting in unison, "Pa-pa! Pa-pa! Pa-pa!"

We scurried out the door to the outside shower, which consisted of a concrete wall and a steel pipe protruding from the wall that spit out just enough water to make do. We knew that with Momma Van coming we had better be clean, or she would give us the Momma smack down. None of us wanted to be enlightened by Momma Van's strong form of persuasion.

After cleaning up a bit and getting a bite to eat, we hurried out to the main entrance. Having someone on "lookout duty" was high priority; everything else would take a back seat to Papa and Momma's arrival. This was Christmas, and we knew that Momma and Papa would make it special.

"Papa! Papa!" we yelled at the first sight of his car. Overwhelming joy bubbled out as we ran alongside the moving vehicle. Papa rolled down his window, and some boys hung onto his hand as he maneuvered carefully down the path. Before long, the car was loaded with boys jumping through the back windows, riding on the back bumper, and climbing onto the hood. "Papa, Papa! Momma, Momma!" we shouted. Our excitement echoed throughout the property. We crowded Momma and Papa's car door, barely leaving enough room for them to squeeze out.

Papa's son, Rick, was also in the car. We loved it when Rick came—he was ever ready for a good game of soccer or an afternoon of silly entertainment. For Rick, language was not a barrier; he had a way of communicating with funny facial expressions and dramatic hand gestures. Laughter was the common language and one we definitely understood.

We loved Papa and Momma Van and could not help but flood them with hugs and welcoming smiles. After helping them carry their luggage into the apartment, we quickly gathered on the front stairs for our fanfare of musical melodies.

We didn't have anything material to give Momma and Papa to show them how much we loved and appreciated them, but we could give them the gift of song. So with the music of the band and the ensemble of our voices, we thanked them. Lifting up through the air were the resounding lyrics, "hoppy welcome to ou, we are hoppy to see ou in me heart." Even though it was not lyrically perfect, it was perfect to Papa—and that was what mattered.

Momma Van wasted no time pulling out our Christmas tree and placing it in the entry hall. She had a bag overflowing with colorful decorations. We took turns placing silver tinsel onto the tree and then added a rope of shiny, chunky red garland. Even though we seldom had electricity, Momma insisted on using multicolored bulbs. After that, we filled the tree from top to bottom with decorative ornaments. Our spectacular Christmas tree transformed the room, turning the surroundings into an explosion of color and holiday cheer.

As the sun melted behind the hut-covered hills, we gathered on the front porch to sing Christmas carols and enjoy our company. Rick was sitting on the stairs relaxing as a few boys massaged his neck, shoulders, and back. Whether he liked it or not, Rick was getting a Haitian spa treatment as each boy fought for his undivided attention. Papa and Momma were resting in wicker chairs we had dragged out from the entryway and placed on the porch.

After relaxing and enjoying the warm tropical breeze, Papa suddenly jumped to his feet, pulled out a large bag from underneath his chair, and loudly proclaimed, "Haiti boys no like candy!"

"Oh yes we do!" we shouted back.

"Haiti boys no like candy!" Papa repeated.

"Oh yes we do," we responded.

And with that, he passed around some tasty treats. This was a real delight—candy was something we loved but rarely had. That evening, we sat with our beloved Papa and Momma with our mouths full of sugar and our hearts full of love.

The next morning, a large truck was parked outside the main building. Papa Van stood near the end of the truck with his hands on his hips. Some boys had gathered around Papa and were peering inside. I was a little curious about what piqued their interest. As I made my way to the truck, I quickly realized it was loaded with one-hundred-pound bags of rice. We promptly made an assembly line that stretched from the back of the truck to the entryway of the orphanage. In no time, the large bags were piled high, overcrowding the entry.

We spent the next few days filling hundreds of small plastic bags with rice and placing them into boxes to await distribution. Reaching out to the community was extremely important to Papa. He simply loved loving people. To Papa, Christmas was the time of year to help others.

In the hot, smoldering sun, with sweat pouring off his brow, Papa stood for hours handing out small bags of rice. He had a well-organized plan: after trial and error, he had found that the best way to distribute the rice was to give it only to children within the community. So that was what he did.

In the past, Papa tried to give the rice to the adults, but the crowd quickly became a crushing swarm of desperate, hungry people rushing the line in a mass panic. Fear of not receiving rice overtook them, and within moments, Papa had to retreat and postpone the outreach. The new method was much safer and more effective. Giving rice to the children not only worked well, but it also ensured that families with more children received more.

I watched in awe as Papa picked up young children and held them in his arms. He could not help but notice their frail bodies; most were malnourished and had swollen bellies. Papa paused for a brief moment, hugged their weak frames, and spoke prayers of comfort. Without hesitation, he scooped up a bag of rice and placed it into their tiny hands. He gently sent them on their way and repeated the same pattern until every bag had been handed out.

As I watched, I wondered what he was thinking. Did he feel like the need was too great? Or did he wonder how could one small bag of rice make a difference in such overwhelming poverty? I never asked him those questions, but one thing was very apparent: he never stopped; he just kept on loving.

Papa Van loved life, and just being with him put a smile on our faces. Celebrating Christmas with him was the highlight of our year. The morning came quickly, and I could hear the sounds of laughter and people talking as the anticipation of our Christmas celebration could be felt throughout the orphanage. The aroma of homemade coconut candy penetrated the air. The sweet scent of sugar, coconut, and Haitian vanilla made my mouth water with delight. Momma Van knew it was our favorite Christmastime treat.

Papa Van was also busy preparing for the festivities, his arms overloaded with gifts that tumbled out of large shopping bags as he scurried through the entry hall. He carefully placed the gifts around the tree, quickly filling the area with colorful Christmas grandeur. In no time we had crowded the foyer, trying to get a glimpse of the Christmas splendor that awaited us.

Papa's voice rose through the air as he sang, "Jingle bells, jingle bells, jingle all the way…" Several of us echoed back, singing it in Creole. The room buzzed with excitement; we could hardly contain ourselves.

Through an interpreter, Papa began telling the Christmas story. His voice rose and fell as he spoke, and we sat in amazement as several boys reenacted Papa's narrative.

Shortly after Papa had finished, Momma Van scooped up the gifts and carefully set a brightly wrapped package in front of each boy. Waiting patiently until each gift was distributed, we laughed with delight in anticipation of what treasures might be inside. As soon as the last present was handed out, the room exploded with Christmastime excitement. Wrapping paper sailed through the air as we frantically opened our gifts and rummaged through bags, pulling out new shorts, shirts, socks, underwear, toothbrushes, toothpaste, and soap. We shouted, laughed, clapped, and celebrated the Christmas abundance. "*Merci beaucoup*," we chanted. What a wonderful blessing!

But Momma Van wasn't finished yet. Oh, no! She continued the celebration, she walked around the room, her arms overflowing with still more, and let each boy pick new pajamas in his size with a matching blanket. Folded carefully within each blanket was our favorite anticipated gift of the season: a wallet. Momma gave wallets to us every Christmas. It was not so much the wallets themselves that overjoyed us, but what was inside. A young lady from Evansville, Indiana, who had challenges of her own would work ironing clothes throughout the year. Tucked neatly inside each wallet was her gift of sacrifice from those earnings: one dollar. Owning a dollar was a very big deal, and it was our most valued gift.

I stood looking at the overwhelming abundance, and suddenly my mom and dad filled my thoughts. How could I enjoy such a celebration when they were barely surviving? I was filled with mixed emotions of guilt and jubilation. While grateful to have been so blessed, my heart ached with the realization that outside our orphanage gates, extreme poverty still ruled their existence.

The aroma of special Creole seasonings, mouthwatering pork, and beans permeated the air. My stomach growled in anticipation, and thoughts of the Christmas feast flooded my mind. We quickly gathered up our gifts and hurried downstairs to stand in line, say our prayer, and take our portion of tasty goodness. We sat in silence, stuffing our mouths with tasty pork and enjoying each morsel. It was pure satisfaction—uninterrupted, finger-licking good, well-fed satisfaction.

As the sun began its brilliantly colored descent, bringing the day to a close, Papa Van jumped to his feet and called out, "Haiti boys no like ice cream!"

"Oh yes we do!" we shouted. In a jiffy, we ran down the stairs and into an old battered van. It took several round trips to get every boy to the ice cream store, but we didn't mind waiting our turn—our bellies were full of overindulgence. With our mouths full of the delicious cream, our voices rang out in unison, "*Merci beaucoup*, Papa; *merci beaucoup*!"

As darkness fell upon the orphanage, I rested my over-stuffed belly, stretching it across my thin, worn-out mattress, and became overwhelmed with emotion. Tears filled my eyes as I recalled the day's celebration, quietly pondering the blessings I graciously had the privilege of receiving. And in the stillness of the night, my heart overflowing with gratitude, I whispered softly, "*Merci Seigneur*; *merci*."

Pursued Opportunity

It was July of 1982, and I was seventeen years old. By this age, we were expected to leave the orphanage. The distress of knowing what was outside the safe haven of the orphanage and that it threatened my existence, burdened the rest of the older boys' minds. The realization of surviving on our own was like a barking dog nipping at our heels. How would we make it in a land of so little opportunity?

Papa never liked letting us go, but with a waiting list of thousands of younger boys needing a home, he had no choice. My day of departure would soon be approaching, and I needed to make some decisions.

I believed that God had my life in His hands. I was strong and knew that I could outlast the hardship of Haiti, but I wanted more. I didn't want to just survive; I wanted to live. I wanted to venture out to a place of opportunity and hope. Never in my wildest imagination could I have known that hope was just around the corner or that the opportunity I had prayed for was on its way.

Dust rose through the air as a van bumped along the rocky road that led to the orphanage. We ran alongside the van, peering in through the windows to catch a glimpse of the anticipated guests. As always, boys rushed the car doors with big, toothy grins and welcoming hugs. We loved visitors. Our excitement grew as we watched Americans, dressed cowboy boots, blue jeans, and pressed, button-up shirts step out. I liked them immediately—after all, I was practically a cowboy myself.

I watched with anticipation as each passenger stepped out of the van. They had traveled all the way from Norman, Oklahoma.

The first was an affluent pastor and businessman named Lee, a tall man with an olive complexion and black hair combed back to one side. He stood strong with a bold demeanor that demanded attention, and he spoke with confidence, not wasting time on useless dialogue. He appeared to be successful, and by the way he carried himself, I could tell he had no trouble getting things done. He remembered meeting me at Papa Van's church when I was younger.

Next came Lee's oldest son, Bryan. He had visited the orphanage several times before, and I recognized him and was delighted to see him again. He had a peaceful demeanor, and it was apparent that he loved the island and the people on it. He was an accomplished musician who led the music department at his father's church. I was immediately drawn to his talent and his love for music. The gift of song still burned within my heart, and it drew me to want to know more about Bryan and his music.

This trip was more than a visit for Bryan; it was an appointment for his family to adopt a child and call him their own. After a few previous visits to the orphanage, Bryan had become fond of one particular boy. The youngster had smooth, light brown skin; long, curly hair; and a bright smile. He had quickly mastered the craft of pulling at heartstrings, so it wasn't long before the boy had captivated Bryan's family.

After Bryan came a married couple who attended Pastor Lee's church. Rick was a large man with a loud, echoing voice who was wearing a cowboy hat, leather boots, and Wrangler jeans. He looked rough, like he was a hard-working man. Sue, his wife, followed closely behind him. She had a small, frail frame and light brown hair that fell right below her shoulders. Her voice was soft and pleasant, and a bright smile lit her face. Beneath Rick's rough exterior was a softhearted cowboy who would jump at any opportunity to help. Sue would just smile and work alongside him, never complaining about the overwhelming task for which he had volunteered them.

As I watched each person exit the van, I could have never realized how significant a role each one would play in changing my life. Why would God bring these people hundreds of miles from their homes to a place of such hardship? Why would they choose to help me—someone they barely knew? God would eventually use each of them to unlock the potential hidden deep within my soul. God had a plan, and once again, He was putting the pieces together.

Before I knew it, I was acting as the Americans' interpreter. I enjoyed speaking back and forth between Creole and English, assisting in communication and helping our guests conduct their business. Interpreting also meant that I was able to travel beyond the orphanage gates and enjoy some adventurous sightseeing while pointing out several locations and explaining Haitian culture and traditions.

One evening as the sun had started to set, the group and I started out on a walk down the dusty path. The village around the orphanage was buzzing with activity. Women wearing shabby headscarves balanced large water pots on their heads as their children laughed and played around their feet. A film of dust rose through the air as merchants packed up their scattered goods.

As we approached the river, the sun was still peeking out from behind the trees, illuminating the scenery below with a soft, warm glow. Several women had tied up their skirts and waded into the river to wash small batches of worn-out garments. Each one had thrown the garments over her shoulders, and taking one piece at a time, she dipped it into the river and rubbed the fabric together to produce soapy suds. They would then rinse and carefully wring out each tattered item and hang it on a nearby tree to dry.

We watched as children and their mothers danced around in the clear water. Mothers soaped and scrubbed their squirming children as bubbles floated down the river, the white foamy suds coming to rest on the riverbank.

Some of the mothers would pick up their tiny babies, hold them in the air, and shout in the direction of the American visitors. "What are they saying?" the Americans asked. As we stood watching the activity, the women would repeat the same actions. I reluctantly interpreted the mothers' desperate pleas: "They want you to take their babies." The Americans gasped in shock and stood in disbelief as I explained how the grave conditions in Haiti and their overwhelming love for their babies left them with no other options. These women were so destitute that many were willing to suffer loss in hopes that their children would have a better tomorrow.

Tears filled our visitors' eyes as the reality of Haiti crashed in around us. Standing on the riverbank, watching the sun as it sank beneath the hut-covered hills, the desperation of the mothers' cries echoed in our ears and overwhelmed our hearts.

The next day brought with it an anticipation of celebration. We jumped with excitement as a rumor swirled around that the Americans were going to bless us with dinner from Kentucky Fried Chicken. It was the only American restaurant on the island, and we were ecstatic that we would enjoy takeout from such a place. We could not contain our joy as we watched the van wind up the rocky road leading to the orphanage.

We flew down the stairs, stood in line, and waited eagerly until every boy was in place for our mealtime prayer. We watched and waited as the Americans carried in the tasty delights, the air filling with the aroma of crunchy goodness and our mouths watering as they prepared each place setting with a heap of crispy chicken. Once dinner was served, we quickly recited our prayer and scurried over to our scrumptious meals.

As we savored the delicious chicken, I could not help but notice the rough and tough cowboy. He stood watching as we devoured our chicken—bones and all. Big tears filled his eyes as he said quietly under his breath, "I want to take them all." The thought of it all softened his rough demeanor as tears poured down his face. He was there to help change Haiti, but in reality, Haiti had changed him.

The generosity of our American visitors and the tasty chicken dinner was etched into our minds as one of the greatest meals we had ever received. We had all experienced a small taste of America, and we loved it.

After spending a week at the orphanage, our visitors were ready for their next adventure: they would be traveling to the coastline of Haiti where the good things of life awaited them. Still needing an interpreter, they asked if I would accompany them. I quickly agreed, and within moments, we were off on our escapade.

Never in my wildest imagination did I think that just several miles from the overpowering poverty sat a hidden paradise, an oasis of abundance in the midst of the misery. I had never seen such beauty. After all this time living in Haiti, I never knew of the riches around the corner.

The endless beauty and sheer elegance of this paradise demanded our full attention. Orange and purple birds of paradise flew among lush tropical greens overlaid with bright fuchsia flowers. A secluded five-star resort with individual beach bungalows sat against white sand and clear, blue-green waters. I could taste the salt on my lips, and the peaceful, calming breeze blew over me as I gazed with wonder at the scene before me.

As the sun melted into the water and engulfed the horizon with a warm, red glow, we sat together on the beach lavishly enjoying soft, ripe avocados and fresh lobster salad. I paused for a moment and thought of Momma and Dad. If only I could summon them to partake in such grandeur. This was like two worlds colliding—one rich and lavish, full of abundance and beauty, and the other filthy, full of hardship and desperation. How could I enjoy the abundant side of Haiti while they were enslaved to its misery? I wanted so much to be a blessing and share with them the beauty I had found within my homeland.

As twilight faded into darkness, I refocused my mind on the opportunity God had placed in front of me. Lee was not only a pastor and a businessman, but he also owned a school. What I wouldn't do for the opportunity to attend school in America! Before I had time to think, I blurted out, "Can I come to your school?"

Without missing a beat, Lee responded, "Yes, no problem. I will take care of everything."

I sat in disbelief. Was it really that easy? A man who barely knew me was willing to invest his time and money in my life. He truly did take care of everything; he paid for my passport and travel expenses and arranged for my educational visa. Through

Lee, God unlocked the door of provision for me. Lee changed my life by giving me hope for a better future.

I soon found myself venturing out to a land of opportunity—an opportunity I called America and a place I would again call home.

Living in America was a dream come true. I was eighteen, and I found myself in the most unlikely place: Oklahoma. Oklahoma was different from Indiana. It was a place of enlightening discovery, with its red dirt, grass-filled plains, and cowboys. Oklahoma was a great place to call home for a "wannabe" cowboy myself. Even though I felt comfortable, never did I think I would live hundreds of miles from everyone and everything that was familiar in America.

My mind raced. Would I ever see my mom and dad again? Would they continue to survive the stresses of Haiti before I could reunite with them? I didn't want to go back to Haiti; there was only hardship there. I wanted to be a blessing. My mom and dad deserved the best, but I had nothing to offer them. My future was uncertain, and I needed to grab every available opportunity, even if it meant stepping into uncharted waters.

The next three years seemed like a rollercoaster ride. I immersed myself in school activities, sports, and music, and I relocated five times, shuffled from one home to another. Church members, schoolmates, and teachers quickly became like family.

The high school I attended was a private school requiring tuition. I worked each day after school washing dishes and cleaning the grounds earning enough to cover the cost. Many times, I found myself missing the fun activities in order to pay for this opportunity. Even though it was hard, I had learned at a young age that good things don't come easily, and the end result is worth the temporary hardship.

I was thankful for the opportunities America had provided, and even though I moved frequently, I was determined to experience everything each family had to offer. I had an open door to a new world, and I was going to walk through it and live.

And not only did I live, but I did so with five exceptional

families.

The Reeds

The Reeds had three daughters ranging in age from eleven to seventeen years old. I was excited to have this new lease on life and grateful for their hospitality. My first night in their home, I quickly settled into bed and caught some shut-eye.

When morning came, the sun peeked in from behind the curtains, and I could hear the girls as they rushed around the house. Their giggles echoed through the hall as I shuffled to the bathroom. Curlers, makeup, and perfume were scattered on the bathroom counter, a colorful rainbow of nail polish and moisturizers lined a nearby shelf, and an assortment of hair products and accessories filled the cabinets. It became apparent that girls ruled this space, and I was a stranger in a new land, captivated by the discovery of a girl's world.

For seventeen years all I had known was an orphanage full of stinky boys, and now I was submerged into a pool of *mademoiselles'* pampered quarters. With so many girls under one roof, I was mothered and nurtured beyond my comprehension.

For six months, this wonderful family cared for me like one of their own. They were kind, hardworking, and loving, and they immediately accepted me into their lives and their family.

The Joneses

After a whirlwind of discoveries, I found myself bunking at the Joneses' house for a month. Life with them was full of fun.

I remember it as if it was yesterday. The warm air was blowing across the field as we huddled together, preparing our strategy. Mr. Jones, a strong ex-boxer, was standing on the sidelines, and his scratchy voice echoed in my ears as he coached the next play. The stands were full of screaming fans, the field illuminated like daytime. With one great throw and a catch from the 50-yard line, I sprinted toward the goal. Mr. Jones stood waving his fist in the air as he yelled and screamed with excitement, "Run, Reeser, run!" and watched intensely as I ran for the touchdown. I understood little about the game, but I was thrilled to be participating in all that America offered.

Our weekday afternoons were filled with football practice, and our Friday nights were occupied with games. There was never a dull moment. The entire family came to the games wearing the team colors and cheering us on as if we were NFL superstars.

The Joneses had three children: an older daughter who was married, a son my age, and another daughter who was a few years younger. The family would gather around the piano as Papa Jones played gospel melodies and his raspy, soulful voice echoed through the air. I joined in with a harmony, making for a wonderful evening of sing-a-longs.

Laughter filled their home and kept me joyfully entertained. Having fun came naturally to them, and their home was filled with silly roughhousing, jokes, and free-spirited kindness. Even though my stay was short, we made memories that still keep me laughing.

The Hills

Shortly after moving in with the Joneses, I found myself spending many nights with the Hill family. They had boys my age, so spending time with them was easy and fun. It wasn't long before they offered me their spare room, making my weekend slumbers more permanent. They already had a full house with five children—two boys and three girls. They must have thought, "What's one more teenager?"

In the mornings, the aroma of fresh baked biscuits, bacon, eggs, and rice wafted into my bedroom. The sun filtered in through the kitchen window as Papa Hill piled the table full with a hearty breakfast, and the smell of them became my alarm clock. Each morning we would gather around the table, laughing and enjoying those delicious meals.

The Hills could not have made me feel more welcome, and living with them was a perfect fit. With that many teenagers under one roof, there was never a shortage of booming music, loud conversation, and rambunctious laughter. We spent late nights watching our favorite show, *The Three Stooges*, slapping our legs, rolling off the couch, and throwing our arms in the air as we laughed uncontrollably at Curly, Larry, and Moe's slapstick comedy.

Comedy was the fiber that weaved through this family. Papa Hill was the ultimate practical joker, and I remember one time in particular when he got me good. He had sat down for dinner and then remembered that he'd left his overcoat in his truck. He asked if I would get it before sitting down for dinner, and without hesitation, I ran outside to the truck. I opened the door and grabbed his overcoat, and my heart nearly jumped out of my chest—under the coat were three large snakes. I sprung back from the truck, slammed the door and ran toward the house, only to see the family peeking through the front window, laughing and pointing at my reaction. My heart pounded for hours afterwards.

I lived with the Hills for two wonderful years. Their joyful attitude and carefree hospitality warmed my heart. They will always be a part of my life and my family.

The Sharps

When the Hill family relocated, I found myself welcomed into the loving home of the Sharp family. Mr. Sharp was a teacher at the school, a church member, and my track coach. He had two sons my age. We ran track together and spent a lot of time with each other, so moving into their home was easy and comfortable. I recall many hot, humid evenings when the track was packed with runners, coaches, and teammates. On one of those evenings, I had made my way to the starting line for the one hundred yard sprint. Coach Sharp watched from the finish line as I stood anticipating the race. At the blast of the gun, I shot out of the blocks and dashed down the lane as my competition nipped at my heels. In the lead, I flew across the finish line where Coach Sharp was waiting with his hand raised for a victorious high five. The smile that beamed across his face said it all. He was proud of me, win or lose, and that made me feel wonderful. "You run faster than a rabbit," he said.

Papa Sharp was such an inspiration to me. He knew a lot about all aspects of life, relationships, sports, and religion—a quality that I found intriguing. During quiet moments in the car or around the dinner table, he would interject advice and wisdom. He listened well, and he inspired me to become the best I could be, encouraging me to reach new heights.

Throughout the six months I lived with the Sharps, I learned that with determination and hard work, I could live my dreams.

I soaked up each and every opportunity. I was doing well and felt blessed to have had the honor to live with such outstanding families. Each one provided for me, cared for me, loved me, and taught me valuable life lessons.

From time to time, I would daydream about my family in Haiti and wonder how they were doing. I never forgot how my parents fought for this moment. They had wanted me to survive, and now not only was I surviving, but I was thriving—thriving in the land of opportunity my parents dreamed about. I was not going to let them down. The weight of saving my family from the clutches of poverty still rested on my shoulders.

My journey was far from over. With a phone call and one simple dinner invitation, my life was about to change forever.

The Williamses

The aroma of fried chicken, mashed potatoes, corn, and fresh rolls permeated the air. Sue's petite frame stood over the stove as she boiled tea bags. With a brief glance, she scurried over to where I was standing, hugged my neck, and offered me a fresh glass of iced tea. Rick, her husband, sauntered over, tilted his cowboy hat, and welcomed me into their home. He had a broad build, wore fresh-pressed Wrangler jeans with brown leather cowboy boots, and sported a red beard that covered the lower half of his face.

I knew them well; they were the couple I had met in Haiti years earlier. Rick and Sue attended Pastor Lee's church and worked with the youth department, so I had spent a lot of time with them and their two children. At that time I was living with the Sharps, who lived a few houses down, but I was often at the Williamses' house watching their two children, Chasti and Chad.

Chasti was nine years old going on eighteen. She had short, curly, strawberry-blonde hair, big brown eyes, and a small, pudgy nose that made the cutest combination, and her larger-than-life personality demanded everyone's attention. She was constantly flipping, doing cartwheels, and bouncing around the house. Five-year-old Chad was quite the opposite. He had short, brown hair, a big bright smile with silver-filled teeth, and a small but powerful physique. He was quiet but always had plenty of hugs and kisses to share.

I was eager to go over to their house that night for dinner. I loved Sue's cooking, which was delicious, and she was an incredible host. The whole Williams family sat around the dinner table—uncles, aunts, children, Ma, and Pa (Rick's mom and dad)—and the mealtime was full of laughter and conversation. Rick sat at the end of the table, loudly sharing a funny story. He had a way of turning an ordinary afternoon meal into a leg-slapping night of entertainment.

After finishing the story, he regained his composure and paused for a moment. He then leaned over the table, looked directly into my eyes, and said, "I want to adopt you. We want you to be a part of our family." I stared for a second in total disbelief. My mind raced, and immediately I said, "I'm too old. I'm twenty; how could I be adopted at this age?" Rick explained that he was good friends with a local judge, and if I wanted to proceed, he could make it happen. He put his large hand on my shoulder and quietly said, "I've seen the way you've gone from home to home, and we want you to settle in and be a part of our family. We want you to have a place to call home and a family to call your own."

After a series of court dates, I was officially adopted. God worked out every detail, even bringing me to a family with my same last name.

For the first time in my life, I had the consistency of a family and a home; I would no longer be moving around, searching for a place to belong. No matter what happened, I now belonged to them. Everything they had was now mine. Wow! It was difficult to wrap my mind around. How could they accept me into their lives and their family?

I was a young black man, now adopted by a white family. What would people think? I had experienced prejudice years earlier in America while living with Momma and Papa Van. At times when Momma and I were shopping around town, people would give us strange stares and make rude comments. I remember being outside at Momma Van's house mowing the yard when a rude passerby shouted, "Nigger!" I ignored it then because I was just a visitor. But now that I was adopted, I was part of the family.

I never wanted someone's ignorant belief system to hurt my adopted family. Rick and Sue were adults and could easily overlook the ignorance, but how would my permanent addition to the family affect their children? The color of my skin never bothered me, but it seemed to be a problem for others. I hoped they could look past their own preconceived ideas and see the heart of a loving family—a family I was honored to call my own.

I knew that Sue had the same concerns. Adopting me was a big decision; after all, she had two other children to consider. But after much persuasion from Rick, she consented. "You trust him with our children, so why would you not give him a home?" Rick had asked her.

Most people in our lives supported Rick and Sue's decision. Occasionally, we would get a stare or a curious question about who I was and how I fit into the family. Generally, though, we just carried on with our daily activities. We were too busy loving life and each other to notice prejudice or inappropriate comments.

Like most families, Papa Rick and Momma Sue both worked during the week. To help out, I spent most of my free time caring for Chasti and Chad. They kept me hopping between school, gymnastics practice, and church activities. I loved every second of it; being together was the highlight of my days. We would laugh and crack jokes as I shuttled them around. As a special treat, we would stop on our route through town to buy ice cream cones or milkshakes.

The weekends were busy with family and friends. Momma Sue would cook up mounds of tasty dishes, filling the house with the fragrances of blended spices, warm sugary vanilla, and buttered delights. She always made an abundance, so we had plenty of leftovers. Papa Rick would entertain with stories of his hilarious daily happenings, his loud laughter echoing through the house. He loved hospitality; the more guests we had, the more he enjoyed it. He would march visitors around the house and property to show them a new project or some recently acquired pet. Being a cowboy, he wasn't happy unless he had a new horse or buffalo to show off.

Life with my adopted family was wonderful. I worked hard to provide for my own things; I was an adult and didn't want to be a financial burden.

Even though I was older, there were plenty of life lessons to be learned. Having lived half my life in Haiti, I wasn't exposed to many of the everyday conveniences that America so richly provided. For example, the use of power tools was foreign to me. I enjoyed fixing things, but I had a more primitive way. Rick would come out of the house shouting, "Boy, what are you doing? Here, let me show you how it's done." I was a quick learner and loved figuring things out.

I also needed to learn about banking and filling out legal paperwork. Rick and Sue were patient, showing me what I needed to do to succeed. I made many mistakes and had my Haitian way of doing things, and Rick would just shake his head and try to keep his composure.

The most valuable thing I learned, though, was how to function within a family. For most of my life, I had moved from place to place, family to family. But this family was permanent and final, and they relied on me and needed me to be a part of their lives. The responsibility of caring for Chad and Chasti, the accountability of belonging—such as letting them know when I would be late—and the unfailing commitment to one another (we always had each other's backs) were plainly taught. The life lessons I learned were instrumental in helping me transform from a boy into a young man.

Because I was older at the time of my adoption, Sue struggled since she didn't have the opportunity to develop a relationship with me while I was young. She didn't experience the precious moments that most moms enjoy with their children as they grow up. Sue felt that our relationship was distant, so she began to pray, "Lord, give me a love for him like I birthed him." Her desire to love me like a mother overwhelmed her. How could she instantly love a grown man she now called her son? God would have to fill her heart with an unconditional love, and that is exactly what the Lord did.

It was early afternoon, and the sun shone down between bright, white clouds in the dark blue sky. I was driving Sue home from the dentist's office, where she'd had a root canal. Rick needed to work that day, so I was happy to help. I felt for her, as she was in a lot of pain and still drowsy from surgery. I gently grabbed her hand and led her into the house, walking slowly through the door and making our way carefully to the couch so that she could lie down.

After experiencing so many surgeries myself, I knew what she was feeling, and I didn't want to leave her side. Every time she woke up, I was there offering a prayer, a kind word, or a song of comfort. I couldn't bear to see her in pain. Although she didn't say much, but I could see in her eyes that she was beginning to realize she could depend on me. Throughout that day, Momma Sue recognized that the love of a mother can come in many forms, and that sometimes, a mom needs the support of her child—and that is okay.

It was 1985—my senior year of high school. Sue had made sure that I participated in all the senior high activities: dances, sporting events, the prom, and get-togethers. I had taken the opportunity to experience American school, and now it was time to bask in the accomplishment. Before I knew it, it was time for graduation. I had made it!

I wished that Momma and Dad could have been there to celebrate this great milestone. Even though many years had passed since I had seen them, I could close my eyes and envision their expressions. Momma would raise her hands to the sky, waving them back and forth as she repeated, "*Merci, Seigneur. Merci, Seigneur*." Dad would stand quietly with his hands behind his back, and big tears would pour down his face as the overwhelming joy became too much for him to contain.

This moment was too great to bask in the glory all by myself; so many people had contributed to my success. As I stood with the diploma in my hand, I remembered the faces of each influential person: Momma, Dad, Papa Van, Momma Van, doctors, nurses, friends, teachers, Rick, and Sue. This was not only my achievement, but rather the accomplishment of so many. This tiny document wasn't just a piece of paper stating that I'd completed secondary education. It was much greater than that—it was freedom. The power of education had freed me from the clutches of poverty.

Life was great, and I had accomplished what I had set out to do—except for one thing. I still battled with the inability to communicate. Due to the massive scar from my previous surgeries, forming words correctly was a huge challenge.

Momma Sue worked for a doctor who worked with a plastic surgeon. "Please take Reeser to go see him—I believe he can help," the doctor pleaded. After performing an examination, the plastic surgeon agreed. "I can't make it perfect, but I can make it much better." And with that, the decision was made. Not only did the doctor agree to perform the surgery, but he would do it free of charge. Once again, I was experiencing an unbelievable financial blessing.

Shortly after the consultation, medical equipment surrounded my bed. An IV bag hung from above while nurses checked my blood pressure, handed me papers to sign, and tucked a warm blanket around my legs. Soon, my eyes became heavy as they surrendered to the drug-induced slumber. Another surgery was on the agenda, but this time it wasn't life threatening.

With my eyes still groggy and my mouth full of gauze, I was wheeled into the recovery room. Momma Sue was waiting with her comforting smile. Bandages covered my bottom lip and chin as nurses checked my blood pressure, removed the IV, and asked about pain. After several hours in recovery, I could finally go home to rest comfortably in my bed.

The surgery was a success, reducing my scar and improving my speech. For the first time in my life, communicating became easy and less stressful.

I felt so blessed to have the consistency of a secure home, blessed to be alive, and blessed to have had opportunities. I recall one particular night at church when I sat pondering the blessings around me, and I was humbled by the act of an incredible man.

The church was full, and soft worship music played, leading us into a time of reflection. As I sat in a chair with my eyes closed, I felt a man's callused hand grab each foot and pull off my shoes. A little startled, I looked down and saw big tears pouring from his eyes and onto the ground. Kneeling at my feet was the rough and tough cowboy I had learned to love—my adoptive father, Rick. He began washing my feet. Emotions flooded over me, and tears poured from my eyes. Sitting in the peaceful atmosphere with my feet submerged in a tub of water, we appreciated the blessing of being father and son.

As I humbly sat there, thankfulness filled my soul to overflowing. The only thing I could think about was how grateful I was to be loved.

1971—Reeser (center) on the front stairs of the orphanage a few months after arriving and before surgery.

Reeser (far left) at the orphanage post-surgery after returning from America.

Reeser (far left) and two other orphans on the front stairs of the orphanage, dressed up for church in the new building.

Reeser (right) with his brother in the orphanage courtyard after surgery, before traveling to Carrefour to visit family.

Reeser with Papa Van in America shortly after surgery. Papa was having Reeser sing at a community event to raise money for the orphanage.

Yves, Angie, and Reeser (right) at Papa Van's house. Reeser was wearing one of his favorite outfits, picked out by Momma Van.

Papa with the boys on the front steps of the orphanage.

An orphanage cook preparing our meal in the kitchen.

Boys holding the Haitian flag for our national anthem at the orphanage school.

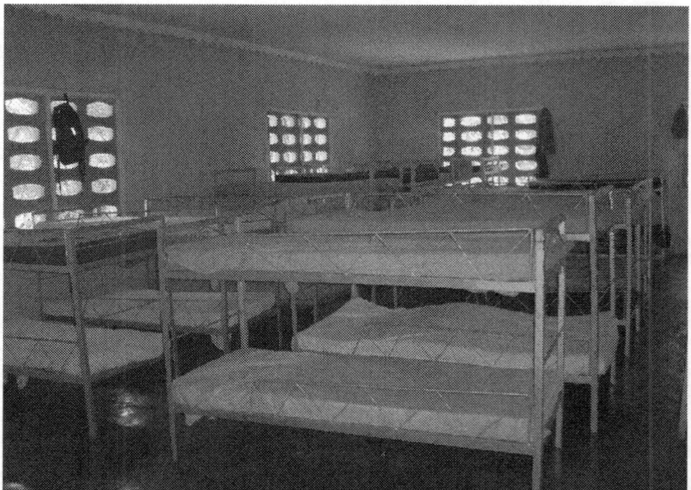

Reeser's room at the orphanage with straw mattresses and iron bunk beds.

Orphans standing on the concrete ramp that Momma Van turned into our slip-n-slide.

Orphans eating in the dining room.

Haiti's outdoor market.

The new church on the grounds of the orphanage.

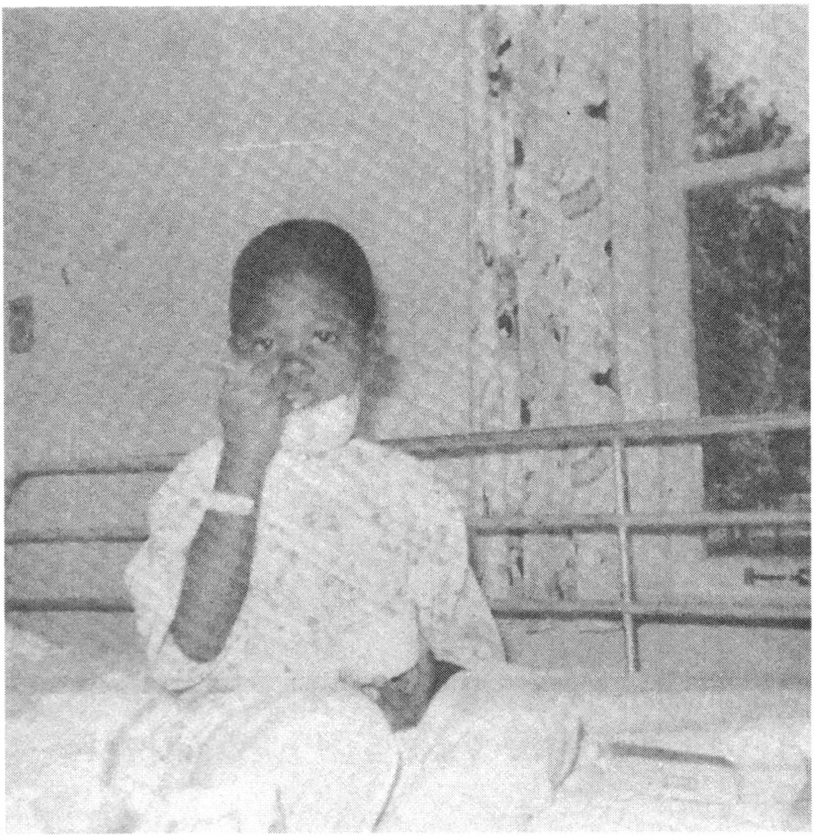

1971- Reeser in the hospital several weeks after surgery, enjoying a tasty treat.

Reeser (front) with siblings and his dad (wearing a hat and holding baby) the first time they saw him after his first surgery. Reeser is holding the small paper bag he had packed for his visit. (His mother is not in the picture.)

Reeser in America with Momma Van, dressed up for their Christmas party.

Boys on the front porch of the orphanage getting ready to sing, "Hoppy welcome to ou."

Reeser (left) in Haiti at the orphanage after his second surgery. Papa had bought one-hundred pound bags of rice for distribution.

A typical house in Haiti.

Reeser in his bedroom at Momma and Papa Van's house, reading *Everything You Need To Know About Becoming a Locksmith*.

The Greatest Gift

God placed many special people in my life who have challenged me, built me up, and helped cultivate my gifts. I recall one evening in particular that changed my life and instilled in me the confidence to fulfill my purpose.

It was a Wednesday night, and I had gone to the midweek church service, which was followed by choir practice. Bryan, Pastor Lee's son, was the music director. One thing that amazed me about Bryan was the way he worshiped. His fingers danced around the keyboard, creating the most incredible melodies. The way he played the piano seemed to draw out the gift of song resting within my soul and made singing easy.

As I listened to the contemporary melodies, my mind wandered back to when I was six years old, the tumor still covering my bottom lip, singing as Momma Van played piano. That had been the first moment I felt the overwhelming presence of the Lord and an unexplainable love for music.

Bryan had asked me earlier that week to lead a song called *Jesus is the Answer*. I will never forget it—just like my experience with Momma Van, I felt the overwhelming power of the Lord saturating my body and anointing my mouth.

As I sang, there was not a dry eye in the choir. Tears poured down my face as I ran my hand over the large scar on my mouth and sang out with total understanding that Jesus *is* the answer. When I lifted my voice, I knew without a doubt that His miracle was the reason I had survived.

From the moment I was born, God had used opposition to propel me into my destiny. A stumbling block became my stepping-stone. Although I was born with the inability to speak or sing clearly, these are the very things God called me to do. There is no doubt that God is behind my success; his undeniable presence empowered my inability and filled my mouth with His song.

I immersed myself in the music program—I couldn't get enough of it. For the next several years, I passionately pursued music under the direction of Bryan and his beautiful wife, Penny. I enjoyed being with them, and we spent our time together composing music. Bryan would sit at the piano, stroking the keys with his gospel flare, while Penny and I sang. Their relentless encouragement was instrumental in developing the gift of song that God had placed in me years earlier.

We often traveled, singing at different venues, and I looked forward to these adventures. I loved meeting new people and exploring unfamiliar places, but nothing could have prepared me for the life-changing introduction I was about to have.

Bryan's father, Lee, had relocated to Arizona and started a church there, and he requested Bryan's musical expertise. Bryan then asked me if I would like to assist with a music conference. The thought of spending a week in Arizona was exhilarating and the opportunity amazing, so I quickly agreed to go.

As the conference began and I stood on the platform, my mind filled with memories of singing in Haiti. I recalled times when I would grab a tin bucket and hit the sides of it with sticks, creating a rhythmic cadence. One of the boys would strum an old guitar with broken strings to create a melody, and with no microphones, we would lift our voices in song. "And look at me now," I thought to myself.

I stood in awe listening to Bryan and an accomplished saxophonist play a new arrangement we had composed for *Bridge over Troubled Water*. As my voice rang out through the sanctuary, I celebrated the gift of song and was grateful for the moment. I never wanted to forget where I had come from and where my mom and dad remained. I knew that whether I was singing with a microphone on a stage with accomplished musicians or singing in

Haiti with a few tattered instruments, the meaning was the same. No matter where I was, God was still faithful, and that is what I celebrated.

After the service, I stood in front of the platform, shaking hands, hugging necks, and reuniting with old friends. Then time seemed to stand still as I met one woman in particular whose big, brown eyes, short, curly hair, and bright smile immediately captivated me. Nervousness swirled inside as I shook her hand and introduced myself, though I was barely able to pronounce my name because she literally took my breath away.

"Hi, I'm Jenny. It's very nice to meet you," she politely said and then walked away.

"She is way out of your league," I thought to myself. I stood there speechless, paralyzed by my nerves. Fear kept me from pursuing her and overwhelmed any sensible reasoning, causing me to miss out on the opportunity of getting to know this remarkable young lady.

I was thrilled when we traveled back to Arizona a year later for another music conference. I prayed that Jenny would attend the music sessions, as I was determined to get to know her better. I had mustered up enough courage to get her number, and we'd talked a few times throughout the year, so I was thrilled when I saw her at the conference and knew that this would be the perfect opportunity.

I invited her to every event that week. We sang, had dinner, went shopping, and spent hours talking, and our time together was incredible. The simple things she did occupied the biggest part of my heart, filling the unknown places. I was in love and felt fully alive. She captivated my attention, and the world around me blurred as her beauty came into full focus.

I couldn't keep her off my mind. I remember Bryan asking, "Hey Reeser, is everything alright? You're being awfully quiet."

"Yes, everything's fine," I replied, but on the inside I was dealing with a thousand butterflies.

On the flight back to Oklahoma, my mind was consumed with thoughts of seeing Jenny again. How could I get back to

Arizona? I wanted to explore our possibilities, but how could I when I was leaving? With one glance she had captured my heart, and now having said goodbye was breaking it. I was crushed, and the fear of not seeing her again overwhelmed me.

Jenny and I didn't see each other for a few years, but even while we were apart, I thought of her often. We kept in touch by phone and through letters. I missed her terribly and prayed that I would see her soon, and before long, God answered my prayer.

In order to help Pastor Lee, Bryan and Penny agreed to move to Arizona to serve as praise and worship ministers. Without hesitation, I jumped on board, ready for the new experience. I wanted to help Bryan, but more than anything I wanted to see Jenny. Thoughts of seeing her again occupied my mind. Would she be excited to see me? How was she doing? Would we feel the same undeniable connection as before? Only time would tell.

I was twenty-five years old and ready to experience life on my own, and the move to Arizona helped me feel independent and empowered. I was excited about the future and ready to take on new challenges. No matter what, I knew God had plans for my life, and I was ready for the adventure.

We arrived to hot desert air that felt like a furnace. Nonetheless, the terrain and southwestern culture of Arizona intrigued me. I liked the opportunity to live somewhere I had yet to explore, and I quickly grew to enjoy the unfamiliar laid-back lifestyle. The hot Arizona climate reminded me of Haiti, making the transition easy.

I set up home in an apartment with a few friends and immediately involved myself with work and music, leaving little time for much else. But even though I stayed busy, I couldn't keep Jenny off my mind. She brought out the best in me and changed my life just by being a part of it. As time went on, our relationship blossomed into a beautiful friendship. I spent most of my time learning about her past and her love for the Lord, enjoying time with her family, and exploring her hopes for the future. We shared a passion for music. The more I learned about her, the more I loved her. She had become my best friend, and I realized in the middle of an ordinary day that God had given me an incredible gift —a gift I never wanted to live without.

We were from two different worlds, coming together and creating our own world of beauty. One reality was full of poverty, hardship and pain; the other was a world of abundance, beauty and sheltered innocence. We were an unlikely pairing enriched by each other's experiences.

We didn't notice the differences in our skin tones or economic situations. We saw the character of our souls and the substance that enriched our hearts.

Our friendship developed into more, and I asked her father if I could date his precious treasure. Her parents had plenty of concerns because of our biracial relationship, but after thoughtful consideration, they gave us their blessing.

Jenny's family accepted me right into their home. Her dad would spend countless hours teaching me mechanical skills while her mom cooked mouth-watering meals. I quickly settled into their lifestyle of movie nights, midafternoon swims, and family outings. They were wonderful people who had raised an outstanding young lady.

After dating for several months, words could no longer express my feelings toward this beauty. In each moment of intense emotional rush, one thing was certain: I needed Jenny in my life. She was a perfect fit. God had created her with me in mind, complementing my character and inspiring me to go beyond what I thought possible. In my life experiences, I knew that it was not so much about what I did that mattered most, but more importantly, who was by my side.

Falling to my knees, I grabbed Jenny's hand. Her big brown eyes filled with tears as I expressed my love for her and told her I couldn't imagine my future without her. With tears streaming down my face, I asked her to become my wife. My heart skipped several beats as I waited for her response, but she looked into my eyes and said, "Yes." She spoke many heartfelt words, but in that instant, the only word I heard was "yes." She was my companion, my best friend, my inspiration, and now she would be my wife.

My love for her was more than a feeling. It was greater than a fleeting moment of goosebumps and butterflies. It was a love that captured my every thought, guiding me to carefully consider each decision with her in mind. I couldn't believe it; God had given me my greatest blessing.

As I stood on the stage, feelings seemed to explode to the surface. This was the day I had dreamed of—I was marrying my sweetheart. Tears poured from my eyes as I quickly regained focus. My voice shook as I could no longer control the overwhelming emotion. As my beautiful bride walked down the aisle, time stood still and the world faded into the background. She took my breath away. I gazed into her eyes as if we were the only two people that existed and softly sang, "I need you, I need you." In that moment of complete transparency, I was captivated by her elegance, never wanting the moment to end.

This was a dream come true. How did I, an orphan, win the heart of such an incredible woman? I grabbed Jenny's hand and held it tightly, as if to say, "I will love you forever." My heart raced as I looked deep into her eyes, realizing that I had the privilege of falling in love with her over and over again throughout our lifetime. In this moment of complete amazement, I knew God had given me a priceless, one-of-a-kind treasure I called my bride.

Our life together wasn't free from challenges. As the saying goes, "Nobody said it would be easy, they just promised it would be worth it." I think this holds true for most people.

Jenny had a way of making me believe I could do anything. She convinced me that the best was yet to come and that together, we would experience it. Even through losing our jobs, going on welfare, and struggling with health problems, we never doubted God's faithfulness. We both believed that life's challenges were just another opportunity for God to perform a miracle.

Jenny had suffered for many years with a medical condition that would make conception difficult. She wept as she explained the complications and the likelihood that we wouldn't have children of our own. As I stood there with her in my arms, I knew that nothing was impossible. God had performed many miracles in my life, and He could do it again.

Each night as we lay in bed, I would place my hand on Jenny's stomach. "Heal every problem, Lord, and give us a miracle," I prayed. After several months, God answered that prayer, and Jenny became pregnant. We were having a baby!

I was filled with fear, excitement, and shock. I knew this was what I had prayed for, but in many ways I didn't feel ready. Would I be able to provide for a baby? The realization of being a papa brought out hidden insecurities. Ready or not, fatherhood was here, and the concerns of being a good dad forced me to an all-too-familiar place—my knees. "Lord, help my shortcomings. I don't want to fail," I pleaded.

The room was dark except for the golden glare of the porch light peeking in from behind the curtains. Labor pains had woken Jenny up hours ago, and now her contractions had gotten much closer. Jenny's body tightened as she felt another stab of pain. Lying still again, she waited with anticipation as another bolt shot across her abdomen. She rose out of bed, pacing the room as the contractions became frequent and rendered her speechless. It was time—our baby was coming! We grabbed her overnight bag and ran out the door.

Within minutes of our arrival at the hospital, Jenny was in a room, and preparation for delivery was underway. Minutes turned into hours—eighteen hours of painful labor, as a matter of fact—until finally, the moment we had prayed for was here. God had blessed us with a healthy baby boy! He was wonderfully created. Standing there in total amazement, I was overwhelmed with emotion. I cradled him in my arms, carefully studying his perfect little toes, dark curly hair, and the baby smooth complexion of his flawless face. Then I noticed he had my lips—lips without a disfigured tumor or scar. And in that moment, for the first time, I felt the overwhelming love of becoming a father. I loved him simply because he was mine.

Standing there speechless as waves of tears flooded my eyes, I realized the heartbreak my dad must have felt that day at the orphanage as he slowly walked the dirt path, leaving me behind. I had hardships, but nothing in comparison to what my father had experienced in order to get me to where my journey began. As I looked down and rubbed my hand over my newborn's tender skin, I wept as I quietly celebrated the joy of fatherhood while also admiring my father's courage and love, letting me go in hopes that I might live. He had left no doubt in my mind of how powerful the love of a father should be.

Even though I hadn't seen my dad in more than ten years, I wanted him to be a part of this monumental moment. I never forgot the sacrifices he made, and to honor his legacy, I named our new arrival after him: Justin. Justin was more than a name; it stood as a reminder of determination, love, and sacrifice.

Holding our precious treasure, I was grateful for the opportunity to pass on the tremendous lessons I had learned. Dad, Papa Van, and Rick were exceptional men, and I was blessed to be their son. As I held my precious newborn, my greatest prayer was that I would be a first-rate father, leaving the same incredible legacy that had been passed down by these three outstanding fathers.

Justin became the center of my world. His dark curls bounced as he tugged at my hand, pleading, "Please daddy, do it again." I chased him around the corner, teasing, "I'm gonna get you!" His loud giggles resounded throughout our apartment as his bare feet pranced against the tile floor. "I got you," I hollered, lifting him into my arms and swinging him around like a rag doll, his high-pitched scream of delight echoing off the walls. "Again, Daddy, again!" he begged. The chase was on—over and over he would peek around the corner, waiting for me to "get" him. I would repeat the game, wrapping him in my arms and blowing raspberries onto his soft belly.

Time flew by, and thoughts of life before Justin became distant memories. He had captivated my attention, changing my world into father-time discoveries. The holidays came to life as anticipation of the season filled our home. Justin's eyes would sparkle as he watched the brightly colored lights. His tiny hands held a bundle of blinking bulbs as he tried to help decorate the

Christmas tree. Jenny placed a few ornaments into his hands, and excitement filled his face as he jumped up and down and placed them onto a few selected branches. He danced around the living room singing along with familiar Christmas tunes.

Even though life was better than ever, at times I would find myself torn between two familiar worlds. Haiti still had its grip, and many times I would find myself feeling guilty for participating in the abundance even while rejoicing in the blessings. How could I enjoy life when I knew the suffering I had left behind? Would I ever feel free from the mental prison? Why should I be blessed when Momma and Dad were barely surviving? I couldn't let it hold me captive. I had to move forward. I wanted to remember them without feeling the pain. And more than anything, I longed for the moment when they could enjoy the blessings, also. Jenny and Justin were too wonderful not to share with them.

Justin was two years old and had more energy than Jenny and me put together. He was full of life and vigor, transforming our lives into early morning snuggle time, peek-a-boo, and butterfly kisses. He brought love into places of my heart I never knew existed.

We made each day a day to remember, creating wonderful family traditions—hiding Justin's Easter basket, watching the Macy's Thanksgiving parade, opening only one present on Christmas Eve and the rest on Christmas morning. I had never experienced childhood traditions, and for the first time, I felt the bond and excitement that these traditions established. This was the family I had longed for. I knew the love of many families, but nothing compared to the bond I felt with Jenny and Justin. They were balm to my soul.

Life was better than I could have dreamed. I was blessed and felt satisfied with God's gifts—but He wasn't finished. Four years after Justin was born, Jenny gave birth to a second child, a nine-pound bundle we named Ben. His dark olive complexion, bright eyes, and dark curly hair captivated us, and we were smitten. His chubby rolls melted into our arms as he nuzzled his face into our necks. His peaceful disposition saturated our souls, filling the corners of our hearts. "How could I love another child as much as I love Justin?" I thought to myself. But I did—I loved him just the same. He didn't need to earn my love or prove he was worthy; I loved him simply because he was mine. As I held him in my arms, I knew that nothing could change my feelings toward him. He was one of my greatest treasures—completely priceless.

The world seemed perfect, but within hours of arriving home, tragedy shook our peaceful existence. I was in another room when I heard my mother-in-law's frantic voice bellowing from the room where the baby had been sleeping, "He's not breathing! Oh, my Lord, the baby isn't breathing!"

In total panic, I rushed into the bedroom, finding my wife and her mother rubbing, pinching, and patting the baby, trying to get a response. Ben's body had gone limp, and he had stopped breathing. Slowly he responded to the stimulation and began breathing again. Our precious Ben was lethargic—no crying and little movement—and we quickly bundled him up and headed back to the hospital. Devastation flooded me as I stood watching doctors poking and probing our newborn, heart monitors and machines surrounding his weakened body. I was filled with hopelessness as I realized there was nothing I could do to help him. I was speechless as I fought with fear. I spoke no elaborate prayer; my mind was overburdened with emotion, and the only word I could muster was, "Jesus!"

For the first time in my life I had a glimpse of the pain that my parents felt on the day I was born. The fear must have paralyzed them. I had the resources of America, yet I could barely breathe at the thought of my inability to help my child. I thought I knew how challenging it was to go through medical emergencies, but when it's your child, nothing can prepare you. Imagining what my parents must have felt when they realized that I would die—something I'd never truly understood until this moment—broke my heart into a billion pieces. As hard as it was, I understood the desperation of the village, wanting to separate from me sooner than later. My mind was flooded with the truth of mortality. The same devastation my parents felt knowing I had little to no chance of survival became all too real.

I wanted to trade places with Ben. I could no longer bear the pain of seeing our infant overwhelmed with needles, tubes, and medical equipment. "Please, Lord, help our son," I pleaded.

After staying several days in the pediatric unit, where Ben underwent countless tests and agonizing blood draws, the doctors determined that our precious newborn had an underdeveloped respiratory system and a small hole in his heart. We were sent home with a heart monitor.

The monitor's alarm would blare through the house with its ear-shrieking alert. Each time, my heart would skip a beat. I would gently rub Ben's tiny body to stimulate his response to breathe. Waiting in anticipation, I stood suspended in time until his shallow breaths started again. The agony of keeping a watchful eye on him left us completely exhausted. Afraid that we would miss an alert, Jenny and I took shifts staying up at night. But thank the Lord, in about two months his respiratory system was fully developed, and he no longer needed the medical device.

Once Ben's medical issue resolved, our world was magnificent and full of little boy wonderment. Our home was filled with toy trucks, rescue rangers, cars, balls, and bats. In the midst of brotherly roughhousing, as the sun sank below the mountains each day and filled the blue sky with rich ribbons of orange, Jenny would fill the tub with bath-time toys. After Justin and Ben splashed around until their hands wrinkled, we lathered them with lotion and slipped them into their superhero jammies, and spent the evening cuddling. And during those moments, the stress of our everyday lives melted into the background, leaving us enriched with what really mattered: Eskimo kisses, slobbery raspberries, and cuddle time.

Several years went by, and life was better than I could have imagined. We were living the dream: a beautiful house, two fantastic boys, great friends, and successful jobs. What more could we ask for? We were experiencing the most in life until, in the midst of an ordinary day, our world was overwhelmed with tragic loss.

We were spending a quiet evening at home when Jenny

suddenly felt pain shooting through her abdomen and stood to her feet. "Something's wrong," she said, while clutching her stomach. "This feels like labor." She reached out for my hand, fear filling her as she realized she was pregnant, and there was no way to stop the waves of contractions that had suddenly flooded her body.

Within thirty minutes, Jenny had miscarried. She wept as she tried to comprehend what had just happened, and questions flooded her mind. Why? What did I do to cause this? She cleaned up, then gently held our baby and placed it into a small container. Gasping for air as tears streaming down her face, she prayed, "Please, sustain me, oh my Lord. I'm overwhelmed with grief." I tried to console my heartbroken wife, but she needed time to process. I held her in my arms and prayed that God would ease her pain.

Several months passed, and much to our surprise, Jenny was pregnant again. She was excited and immediately started planning for the new arrival. She was hopeful that this would be the baby girl she had prayed for, but either way, we were thrilled to be having another little one.

After a doctor's appointment, she pranced through the door with her arms loaded with packets of information, a diaper bag, samples of baby wash, and formula. She was ecstatic with the news that everything looked good. After a few months of morning sickness, hormonal changes, and tight-fitting clothes, she was confident her pregnancy was right on track.

Weeks went by, and it was time for Jenny's next doctor's visit. I got ready for work while Jenny prepared for her appointment. She put away some dishes, straightened up our bedroom, and kissed me goodbye.

I arrived at work and was welcomed by piles of paper cluttering my desk. I was working on the mound of priority tasks when I received her call.

"Hello, hon," I said.

Sobbing was all I could hear as Jenny tried to control the heart-wrenching distress.

"What's wrong, honey?" I asked.

Her voice shaking, she answered, "There's no heartbeat. The

doctor found no heartbeat!"

I was speechless, and in this moment of despair, the only words of comfort I could offer were, "I love you. I am so sorry."

"I know," she whispered.

The painful reality cut into my heart. I was at a loss as to how to provide comfort. I knew her heart was broken into a billion pieces, and there was no way I could put it back together. She would need time to process the loss of another baby, and only God could heal and ease her grief. Even though she never had the opportunity to hold this child, she had cradled the baby within her heart.

Jenny tried to put on a brave face to avoid upsetting our other two children, but the grief was consuming. Looking for a secluded spot while the boys played in the living room, she sat in our bedroom, struggling to fight back her tears. She tried to regain her composure, counting down the minutes until I returned home, but she couldn't stop the tears. The more she tried to fight the rush of emotion, the stronger it came. A few minutes later Justin peeked through the door and walked slowly to where his mom was sitting.

"Why are you crying, Mommy?" he asked. He sat down beside her, his face turned upward. "Mommy, what's wrong?"

She wiped the tears from her face. "Oh, sweetheart, Mommy is sad because the baby in my tummy went to heaven to be with Jesus."

His little hand reached across gently wiping his mother's tears. "Oh, Mommy, I'm sorry," he said. "Everything is going to be okay."

"I know, sweetheart. You don't worry; Mommy is okay," she replied.

In that moment of complete heartbreak, she thanked God for the blessing of motherhood, even if it meant experiencing such pain. She knew that other people may forget the loss, but a mother's heart never does. In order not to neglect the life that was lost, she named our baby Olivia, which means peace. She knew that peace would live forever, and it would remain in her heart.

As hard as I tried, I couldn't find the words to comfort my wife. I was grieving, too, and knew that the only way to process this hardship was through prayer. Closing myself off to the rest of my family, I poured my heart out. God had gotten me through tragedy before, and I knew He would do it again. Our loss had devastated me, but despite my heartbreak, I needed to stay strong. Comforting Jenny was foremost on my mind, and I knew that only together would we get through this.

Shortly after this second miscarriage, Jenny experienced more medical problems and, due to the risk of having more miscarriages, Jenny decided a tubal ligation would be the best option. I knew her heart was crushed by the prospect of never having another child. She loved being a mother and dreamed of sharing the bond that comes from having a daughter. It seemed that mother-daughter dress-ups, tea parties, pink ruffles, and prom dresses would never be. But she was extremely grateful for the two little miracles who ran through the house and thanked God every day for her greatest blessings.

A beautiful mixture of colors filled the sky as the sun sank below the horizon. The mountains stood tall, surrounding the valley with spectacular colored rock formations. It was June of 2000, and Jenny and I were zooming through the valley, excited about meeting Rick and Nancy VanHoose for dinner. They were in town for several days, taking in the Arizona sights and enjoying some summertime poolside relaxation.

Conversation and laughter filled our time at dinner as we enjoyed each other's company. Rick's hilarious stories kept us in stitches as we sat on the edge of our seats, prompting him for more. Soon, though, the conversation grew serious as Nancy discussed her adoption agency. Nancy had started a successful ministry working with women in crisis pregnancies and placing their babies into loving homes. Her compassion and wisdom had touched countless lives. On this particular evening she told us about a mother who would be giving birth to a baby girl the following month who needed to be placed with an adoptive couple. Given that the baby's arrival was coming so quickly, the pressing need to find a loving home was forefront on her mind. Jenny looked across the table at me, and without her saying a word, I knew what she was thinking. The desire to have a baby still remained within her heart. In silence she listened to the conversation as her painful loss transformed into a desire to adopt. Jenny sat in awe as God's bigger plan for our family started to unfold.

At home later, Jenny shared with me her revelation. "Maybe God has it in His plan for us to adopt this baby girl. Why do you think they haven't found an adoptive family when people are lined up for miles wanting to adopt a precious newborn?" Jenny pleaded.

Not letting me get a word in edgewise, she kept speaking. "Our baby was due the exact time this baby is due. Do you think that's just a coincidence? I really want this baby—a beautiful baby girl—what a blessing."

After exhausting her plea, she sat down and waited for my response. She had been through a lot, and she was overwhelmed emotionally. I thought if I could calm her down, she would understand my concerns and come to her senses.

"Honey, I understand that you want this baby, but there's no way we can adopt," I calmly stated. "Adoptions take thousands of dollars. I am so sorry, but it would take a miracle. There's no possible way we can afford this," I responded.

Jenny looked at me, her brown eyes flooding with tears that poured down her face. "I know it costs a lot," she stated. "I guess I was hoping for the impossible."

After our conversation, Jenny went into our bedroom, and with her head buried into the mattress, she cried out in despair. "Lord, you said that you would give us the desires of our heart." Tears soaked into the blanket as uncontrollable sobs rushed out. "If it be Your will, please grant me my desire. Please hear my cry." Heartbreak came up from the deepest part of her soul as she pleaded, "I want this baby girl, and I believe that You, my Lord, can make it possible."

The last few months had suddenly crashed in around her: the loss of the babies, then the hope of adopting and the devastation of realizing that we had no financial way to make it possible inundated her soul. She needed God to hear her most intimate thoughts and heal her deepest wounds. She battled with her emotions, fighting through to make her request known to the Lord until finally finding peace, and in the stillness of the night, she knew that God had heard her cries.

The next morning, the world was quiet as the sun rose over the mountains, painting the sky with pink ribbons. It was Sunday, and Rick would be preaching at church. I loved being in service with Rick and Nancy, because it brought back memories of living with Papa Van in Indiana. They were family, and spending time together was something I cherished.

The church service started with a celebration of praise. The choir rocked from side to side and clapped as they sang a fast-paced melody. I loved watching Nancy as she grinned from ear to ear, enjoying the uplifting praise. After the choir finished, Nancy greeted the congregation and told the story she had shared with us the evening before about the baby girl who was soon to be born and needed a forever family. I knew that in this church of more than three thousand people, there was sure to be several couples who would be perfect matches. Before she could finish, Pastor Lee interrupted by walking up onto the platform. He pointed directly at my wife and said, "You want this baby, don't you?"

Immediately, tears filled Jenny's eyes as she sat in complete shock. I wondered how he possibly could have known that Jenny wanted the baby when we hadn't told anyone.

"Yes, she does, but we can't afford it," I quickly responded. I couldn't believe this conversation was taking place in the middle of the service.

Without hesitation, Lee looked at me and said, "Money is not a problem; we'll see that it gets taken care of. If you want this baby, we'll make it happen."

Just like that—I couldn't believe it! Tears streamed down our faces as God provided from heaven once again, captivating our hearts. It took several minutes to comprehend the magnitude of what had happened. The night before my wife had pleaded to the Lord, and He heard her cries. This morning, He gave her the desire of her heart. We were to experience the miracle of adoption.

I'll never forget the first time I saw our precious baby girl. I stood in amazement, staring at her angelic features—tiny hands, perfect lips, and baby-smooth skin. White satin and lace ruffles covered her little body. From the moment they placed her in my arms, she snuggled right into my heart. She was perfect. Tears blurred my vision as I thanked the Lord for our beautiful daughter. She was sent from heaven—hand-picked for us by God. To honor this blessing He had given us, we named her Madisen, which means "gift of the Lord."

It was love at first sight. She settled right into our family, and Jenny quickly settled into mother-daughter bliss. Bows decorated Maddy's black, curly hair, ruffles overwhelmed her petite frame, and bracelets sparkled on her ebony skin. Maddy brought little-girl pizzazz, filling our once little-boy home with sparkles, baby dolls, princesses, and everything pink.

I never could have imagined how wonderful my life would be. God had given me the opportunity to adopt this beautiful child, just as I had been adopted. God had rescued me, and now He had given me the opportunity to do the same for her. We were blessed, Madisen and I; we shared a special bond that came from being given up—because of love—by mothers who hoped that this might give us better futures. Madisen was a priceless treasure, and I was honored that God had chosen me to be her father.

I was rich—rich with love! It came from every direction and revealed itself in the faces of my beautiful family. It was represented in my mom and dad in Haiti. Love reached out through Papa Van, transforming my very existence. Compassion had touched the heart of a rugged cowboy who adopted me so that I could have the security of a future and a sense of belonging. And love had brought me Jenny—completing my life with companionship, intimacy, and three wonderful children.

I realized that love was a choice, and I thanked God that these precious people had chosen me.

Back Home

After many years of living in Arizona, we relocated to Oklahoma to be closer to my adoptive family. Rick and Sue were delighted to have their grandchildren close by. We quickly settled into the heartland's lifestyle of football, family dinners, and country comforts.

Although I was grateful to be around family, I felt unsettled—restless in my spirit with the desire to experience more in life, like a ship being tossed about in a storm. I questioned the move to Oklahoma, my decisions, my abilities. How did I go from being on top of the world to feeling lost in the wilderness? I didn't understand why I was feeling this way. But then God gave me direction and clarity.

Through a series of connections, my family and I found ourselves traveling six hours each weekend to Bartlesville, Oklahoma, to lead praise and worship. As soon as we arrived at the friendly spirit-filled church, we felt at home. Jenny and I had always been part of a music program, but we had little experience teaching music and leading a congregation. To our surprise, the musical challenge came easy. I felt reassured, confident, and satisfied, and within moments, I knew that this was what I was born to do.

So we drove the long distance, back and forth each weekend for eight months, until the traveling took its toll on us. Since I was now certain about my future, we decided to relocate to be closer to the church. God had been preparing me for this moment my whole life. He never puts us in a position unless we're ready, and He had surrounded me with exceptional people who spoke into my life, teaching me about leadership, character, and skill. I was being shaped and stretched into the leader that God wanted me to be.

It wasn't all glorious. I had plenty of growing pains, and we worked full time jobs while serving as worship leaders, but the outcome of each new challenge left me overjoyed with the realization that I was living out God's plan for my life. I not only had the pleasure of serving as a music minister, but we had the privilege of ministering together as a family. With my wife on the piano, Justin on the drums, and Ben on the bass, we praised the Lord together.

The busyness of life didn't keep me from thinking about my family in Haiti, though. I often wondered if my parents were still living. If so, how were they doing? I knew that I was blessed in my present and my future was bright, but I never wanted to forget my past. At times I still felt guilty for having so much while they were enslaved to poverty.

But I was afraid to return to Haiti. After all, I had been delivered from there; why go back, only to find my family living in misery? What could I do to change it? These questions disturbed and sometimes overwhelmed me, and the only thing I could do was pray for my family's well-being.

We had been living in Oklahoma for several years when I received a phone call from Bryan, who told me he was going on a mission trip to Haiti. He hadn't been there for over twenty years. I was excited he was going; perhaps he could find answers to some of my pressing questions.

"Would you try to find my family? I know it's a shot in the dark, but it's worth a try," I asked.

"Of course!" Bryan responded.

Excitement and fear welled up inside as I thought about the overwhelming challenge of finding my family. It would be like trying to find a needle in a haystack, since I had no idea of their whereabouts. I hadn't spoken to them for more than twenty years, so I didn't know what Bryan would find or what news I would receive.

One quiet afternoon as Jenny and I were resting in our living room, the phone rang. It was Bryan, calling from Haiti. After exchanging greetings, he said, "You'll never guess who's standing in front of me."

"Is it my family?" I asked expectantly.

"Yes, it's your family," Bryan responded.

Laughter, excitement, and tears bubbled up in me. "My mom—is she there?" I asked.

"Yes, Reeser, your mom is still alive. Your brothers, their wives, and their children are here, too."

I couldn't believe it. Jenny and I laughed and cried, unable to say anything. How in the world, with no electric, no phones, and no resources other than word of mouth, did Bryan find my family? And my mom—she was alive! My father had passed away, but my mom was a survivor. I stood motionless, trying to process the fact that my family had been found and that despite the odds, they had survived.

Jenny looked at me and finally said, "I know you need to get your American citizenship before you feel safe traveling to Haiti, but I can't wait. I'm going to Haiti to meet our family." And within a few months, she was on her way.

Jenny traveled to Haiti with a large group, along with Rick, Bryan, and Penny, so I knew she was in good hands. She had collected dresses, shoes, jewelry, soap, lotion, blankets, and other necessities to bring with her. She was delighted for the opportunity to meet my—our—family, and she wanted to be a blessing.

A few hours after arriving at the orphanage, Jenny was busy working when a boy came barreling through the door, telling her, "You have a visitor." Immediately, Jenny knew who it was: my mother.

The woman who had fought for my life was waiting to meet her. She was the mom who had not seen or heard from her son in over twenty years. How would my mom respond? Would she accept Jenny, or would she reject our efforts? Fear gripped my wife and she tried to regain her composure. She wanted to be accepted as a daughter, but with so many unanswered questions, she was unsure. Walking down the long, narrow hall to the main entrance, the thought that "love never fails" inundated Jenny's soul, reassuring her that all she needed to do was extend love.

My mother was sitting on a wicker bench. She wore a blue dress, and her hair was tied back into a well-used scarf. Her shoes were worn, and her skin looked dry, as though she had walked several miles along dusty roads. Jenny knelt at Momma's feet, took her hand, and gently kissed each cheek as she greeted her with, "*Bonjour*."

"*Bonjour*," Momma replied.

Tears poured down my wife's face as she held her mother-in-law's hand. Her hand was dry and callused from hard work; her face was rough and wrinkled from the harsh sun; her eyes were red from the dusty roads; and her frail body spoke of years of difficult labor and poor nutrition.

Jenny spoke through an interpreter, "I've brought you a video—it's a video of your son and your grandchildren."

Jenny knew that this moment was going to be life changing. My mom was about to see me for the first time in more than twenty years, and she had never seen her grandchildren. The room grew still as Jenny turned the video camera toward Momma, who held the camera close to her face, hanging onto each word and every image displayed.

"These are my grandchildren?" she asked.

"Yes, they are," Jenny responded.

Watching intensely, never taking her eyes off of the video, Momma asked, "What are their names?"

"You have two grandsons, Justin and Ben, and a granddaughter, Madisen."

"Justin, Ben, and Madisen," Momma repeated.

Tears welled up in her eyes as she watched the video, taking a deep breath as she listened to my recorded self, telling her that I loved and missed her. Holding the video camera inches from her face, she studied my image.

"Louissaint," she said.

The tears now poured from Momma's eyes as she listened to my voice. Her son was alive and well! Everything else around her disappeared; the only thing she cared about in that moment was her son.

"Reeser couldn't travel this time because he needs the proper paperwork. As soon as he gets it, he'll come. He wants to see you," Jenny explained.

Momma nodded her head as if to say, "I understand."

Jenny was very excited to share with Momma the treasures she brought. It was very apparent that my Haitian mom had very little, and the thought that we could be a blessing thrilled my wife. Still kneeling at Momma's feet, my wife described the luxuries she had brought her. "We want to bless you and buy you the things you need," Jenny explained.

Jenny knew Momma didn't have a bed, running water, furniture, or electricity. The magnitude of the need took her breath away, and the little that we could do diminished in comparison.

"What do you need? What would you like to have?" Jenny asked.

Momma reached out and put her hands on the sides of Jenny's face. With a gentle sigh, looking directly into Jenny's eyes, Momma said, "I need to see my son. I need to see him face to face."

Jenny was overcome with emotion, and time stood still for her as she looked into the eyes and heart of my mother. Nothing could compare to the desperate need to see her son; no amount of money could replace her desire to be with me. Her love transcended the poverty, the lack, and the need, welling up from deep within her soul. She appreciated the monetary goods, but there was nothing she needed more than to see her son face to face.

Jenny's trip to Haiti changed her, and she came back to America determined to reunite a mother and her son. She understood the importance of relationship. While material things come and go, people are what really matter. Truly being blessed is the bond we share with each other—blessed to be able to invest our time, support, and love into the lives of others. Jenny knew that the greatest treasures were found in the hearts of our family and friends, and nothing on this earth was more valuable than the people we loved and the blessing of having them in our lives.

"I promised Momma that you would see her again, and that was the only thing she asked for," Jenny would remind me. Through my wife's perseverance, I was soon on my way back to Haiti to fulfill our promise.

Haiti

The smell of coals burning from the open fires brought back a flood of childhood memories. I hadn't been to Haiti for so long, and this time it was very different: I was traveling back as a visitor, not a resident. It felt freeing yet burdensome; the freedom brought with it a sense of obligation—an obligation to be a blessing, because I had been blessed.

I looked out at the familiar landscape of rocky roads and congested markets as our van slowly maneuvered through Port-au-Prince. Instead of staying at the orphanage, I would be at a nice hotel with upscale amenities. I came to see my Haitian mom, and I was going to give her the good life, even if only for a week.

I was to meet Momma at the orphanage; I would be there during the day, working on repairs and visiting the children. My stomach churned with nerves as the anticipation of seeing my mom flooded my mind. I was still a child the last time I saw her, and now I was a man with children of my own. Even though years had passed since I had seen my mom, my love for her never wavered or waned. After all these years, her love, approval, and acceptance were still important to me. She was my mom, and I needed to see her face to face as well.

The sunbeams danced through the dust-filled air as the boys' laughter echoed throughout the large concrete building, the warm, tropical air rushing through the partially screened windows. I knew Momma would arrive soon, so I occupied my mind with making repairs. In no time, an orphan ran into the room, announcing that my family was here. Immediately, emotion surged through my body. As I walked toward the front entry porch, my heart felt as though it would pound out of my chest.

I rounded the corner and caught a glimpse of Momma sitting

on a wicker chair. A light-colored dress hung on her fragile frame, and her straw hat cast a shadow across her face. Before I knew it, I was running toward the elderly woman I recognized to be my mom. Seeing me, she gasped and jumped forward, trying to stand, only to realize that her weakened body could not respond. Falling back into her chair, she reached out, we met in an embrace. Her thin arms wrapped around my back and held me tightly, as if to say, "I never want to let you go."

I wept as my mom held me, rocking me back and forth as though I were still the little boy she remembered. The reassurance that she had never forgotten me and that she still loved me flooded my heart. Taking a deep breath, I soaked it all in. It was therapeutic. Our love and bond transcended time, reaching beyond the years we had lost.

We held each other, speechless, as tears poured down our faces. This was the answer to my mother's prayer, her desire to see me again that rang upon the ears of her Creator. My mother's love had compelled her to let me go, and now that same love had brought me back.

I recognized the faces of my brothers and sisters as they crowded around the front porch of the orphanage. They were small in stature, and their smiles and bright eyes welcomed me. My brothers immediately grabbed me and greeted me with *bonjours*, kisses, and strong hugs. Joy filled me as I noticed with disbelief how much we looked alike. I laughed at myself when I stumbled over my words, trying to regain the memory of a language I hadn't spoken in years. My sisters gathered around, too, hugging my neck and holding my hand.

I had twelve brothers and sisters, so there was no shortage of family greetings. Smaller children danced around our legs as my siblings introduced my nephews and nieces. "This is my family," I laughed to myself. A beautiful mixture of culture, love, and heritage was represented in each face. It didn't take long to rekindle family bonds as we reminisced about childhood adventures and updated each other on life's monumental events.

The day was filled with laughter, affection, and overwhelming gratitude. I was thankful for family and for the privilege of having each one of them in my life. All too soon, though, the darkness of night crept over the island terrain, and before the sun made its final departure, we said our farewells for the night as Momma and I left for the hotel.

I had only one week to lavish my mother with modern conveniences, so each moment was significant. Jenny couldn't come with me on this trip, but she had packed a bag with items with which Momma could pamper herself—powder, lotion, perfume, bubble bath, slippers, and a satin nightgown—and given me specific instructions on how to give my mom a relaxing, spa-like experience. My wife knew that Momma had never experienced the pleasures of running water or indoor plumbing, so she wanted her first time to be extra special.

Once at the hotel, we gathered our luggage and proceeded up a flight of stairs to our room. As we entered, Momma and I were greeted with pure luxury, a retreat hidden away from the world to which Momma was accustomed. She gazed around the room, taking in the marvelous abundance, a smile filling her face as she waved her hands to the sky. With each new discovery, she murmured, "Oh, ooh...." I believe the experience left her speechless.

Her attention was drawn to the focal point of the room: a king-size bed with fluffy pillows and luxurious linens. I held her hand and carefully helped her onto the mountain of softness. She rested against the silky fabrics and ran her hand gently across each side of the bed, feeling the comfort. This was the first time she had laid her head on something so plush. The realization that my mom slept on dirt floors and torn-up rags was more than I could bear, and tears streamed down my face. My mom lay there taking in the abundance, and in the quiet of the evening, she raised her hands to the sky, waving them back and forth proclaiming, "*Hallelujah! Merci, Seigneur; merci!*"

After absorbing the magnitude of the moment, I quickly made a decision. I picked up the phone to call the front desk, and I ordered a rollaway cot; my mom was going to enjoy having the oversized, luxurious bed all to herself. That made me smile.

After the initial shock of seeing the room, I thought it fitting to give her the luxury Jenny had sent. While Momma rested, I prepared a relaxing experience for her in the bathroom. I ran a warm bath in the large red clawfoot tub, set out powder and lotion, and placed Momma's slippers next to the tub. Momma shuffled her way into the bathroom while I waited outside the door.

A puddle surrounded Momma's feet as she stood on the white tile, splashing water over the side of the tub. "Momma, get into the tub. Sit down and relax!" I yelled through the partially opened door. This time, Momma stepped into the tub, stood there, and splashed the water up as if she was in a river. She had no idea how to relax in a bathtub; she had bathed out of a bucket or in a river her entire life. I could not help but laugh as water puddled on the bathroom floor. "So much for the spa experience," I said to myself.

Momma finished cleaning up, put on her satin nightgown, and showed off her pink fuzzy slippers. I had already tried the bath experience without success, so getting her into a proper outfit for dinner was more than I could handle. Momma accompanied me that evening in her satin nightgown and fuzzy slippers.

As the week came to a close, my heart was grieved with thoughts of saying goodbye. It's never easy, but leaving my Haitian mom was extremely difficult. She was frail and elderly, and she'd lived a strenuous existence. If I could ease the hardship of her everyday life, then that was what I wanted to do. Tears poured down her ebony face as she held onto my hand. A surge of emotions crashed through my heart like a stormy sea pouring out through the windows of my soul. As I watched her frail figure step into the taptap, I was tortured by the thought that within moments, a sea of impoverishment would overtake her, and I would be consumed by the desire and inability to make things better. The reality of Haiti made saying goodbye torturous. There had been little in my life that compared to the pain of leaving my mom behind that day.

While I was glad to be home once again in Oklahoma, reuniting with my Haitian family had changed my perspective and set me on a new path. I felt a strong calling to return to where I had begun. I needed to go back to Evansville, Indiana.

Papa Van's son, Rick, was the pastor of The Cathedral, the church that Papa had started more than seventy years ago. The church had supported the orphanage for more than fifty years, and now my heart was being drawn to the same ministry that had impacted my life so dramatically.

For years, Pastor Rick had regularly asked when I was coming home. I would just laugh, not taking him seriously. After a few years of hearing the same question, though, and a conversation with Rick during a visit to Indiana, I realized that that was where I needed to be. Before long, we had made Evansville, Indiana, our new home.

Jenny and I were honored to serve as praise and worship ministers. We were blessed to work with musicians who sang and played not only with skill, but also with surrendered hearts. It was more than I could have dreamed.

I looked at the familiar faces from my childhood and could not help but raise my hands to the sky as passion exploded with the realization that, at the age of six, God had called me here. Emotion flooded over me as I remembered the first time Momma Van stood me on the platform to sing. As I looked out over the congregation, I was overtaken with thoughts of Momma and Papa Van. They had since gone on to be with the Lord, but their legacy lived on in Rick, Julie, and me.

As I stood there, I wondered if Papa Van saw the reward of his labor forty years ago, when I was an impoverished orphan from Haiti. Did he envision this day? Standing there lifting my voice toward Heaven, leading the people into worship, I was sure that God had pulled back the heavens, silenced the angels, and let Momma and Papa Van participate in this celebration of praise. This moment was solely about the goodness of the Lord and the legacy of His servants.

I was honored to be back in Evansville with the people who had supported and prayed for me when I was a child, now leading them in worship, thirty years later. Who would have thought that God would use the inability of a small child, unable to speak English and with a tumor holding his mouth captive, to glorify

Him? But that is the amazing God we serve. I'm honored that each time I open my mouth to sing, it's evident that when God is in it, anything is possible.

Momma

By all accounts, I was blessed: a beautiful wife, three fantastic children, and a success story. But even with a life story full of miracles, triumph, and wonder, my heart was heavy with the burden of my Haitian mom's existence. Her hardships rested upon my shoulders—a load I was willing to bear.

Jenny and I made several trips to Haiti, each time bringing essential items to lighten the load of surviving Haiti's reality. My mom and family were grateful for the blessings, but each time it became harder to say good-bye. The difficult formalities of processing Momma's visitation visa left me powerless when she asked to come to America, and I was devastated. I knew it broke her heart.

Her calloused hands covered her face, burying the heart-wrenching sobs that erupted from the deepest part of her soul. She needed to empty the heartbreak; a lifetime of adversity poured from her eyes.

Fountains of tears streamed down my face, too, as I stood there thinking, "No point in wiping them—let them fall." My heart shattered into a billion pieces, as I could do nothing to console her despair. I could no longer bear the heartbreak of leaving Momma behind. I was determined.

Six months later, after much grueling paperwork, Jenny and I rejoiced when Momma received her visitation visa. She would finally be coming home with me! Jenny and I fixed up a bedroom and planned for her stay in America. We were thrilled that Momma finally had the opportunity to experience the blessings that our home offered. We wasted no time making travel arrangements, and before I knew it, I was soaring through the blue skies, headed back to Haiti. This time there would be no good-bye. Momma would be making America her new home.

The daylight peeked in through the windows, announcing the start of a monumental day. Momma had wasted no time, and she now sat at the end of the bed, staring at me as though I was slowing her down. She was on the threshold of a new journey. Anticipation had driven her imagination to a land of abundance, and now she needed her body to catch up to where her mind had already taken her. The morning could not move fast enough.

She gripped my hand tightly as we maneuvered through the crowded streets. Getting to the airport was not an easy task, as pedestrians, taptaps, and merchants crowded the dirty roads. When we finally arrived, I grabbed our luggage, held Momma's hand and led the way through the checkpoints. She followed closely, eyes as big as saucers as we filed onto the plane. Taking our seats, I reached across to buckle the seatbelt on her. She grabbed my hand, squeezing tightly as the plane roared down the runway. Taking a deep breath, she looked over at me; she was completely terrified. I remembered feeling exactly the same years earlier when I would travel with Papa Van. At the age of 76, she had only ridden in a vehicle a few times, and now she was plunging through the sky like a speeding rocket. I gave her a reassuring smile and tried to soothe her nerves.

After a couple of hours, we glided down onto the landing strip and into Momma's new world. She had finally arrived in America! Customs, checkpoints, and fast-paced arrivals and departures confused Momma, and I had to keep a watchful eye on her. She was like a child as she experienced this new world for the first time. The simple task of riding an escalator turned Momma into a contortionist. We looked like a circus act as I fumbled with luggage, Momma, and the moving stairs, and I laughed out loud as Momma hung on for her life, riding with her legs stretched three feet apart. As we approached our next plane, I took a deep breath to regain any dignity and thanked God that we were finally on the last leg of our journey.

Family and friends greeted Momma as she sauntered down the long hall of the Evansville airport. Even though she couldn't understand the spoken language, the display of love was crystal clear. Smiles, hugs, and handshakes overwhelmed Momma as she took in the unfamiliar surroundings.

Momma had spent the majority of her life dreaming about the land of opportunity, and she had finally arrived. She was a stranger in a land of abundance, overindulgence, and convenience. Nothing was common—not the language, the food, or the culture.

Each day held a new surprise as Momma explored this foreign world. The sounds of the washing machine puzzled her, as she was used to washing clothes in a river or bucket and hanging them on a nearby tree to dry. A switch that could be flipped up and down to light a room was inconceivable, and she often sat in the dark. Faucets that turned on and off to provide clean water left her confused, and she would often leave water running in the sink.

As I watched Momma discover the abundance that I took for granted, I was humbled. How could I ever again complain about trivial things when, for seventy-six years, my own mom had walked several blocks to use a public outhouse that was nothing more than a hole in the ground and had never flushed a toilet or had access to toilet paper? Even sitting at a table to eat dinner was a new experience, since she had never owned a dining table and was accustomed to putting her plate on her lap. Oftentimes Momma would toss what was left onto the kitchen floor or throw her trash onto our living room carpet. Jenny would laugh and pick it up, and I would remind Momma that we put unwanted items in the garbage can. She was like a youngster learning things for the first time.

It was a delight having Momma in my home. I loved her, and wanted to share with her the abundance of America so that she could experience the pleasures I had come to enjoy. Her life of hardship and impoverishment had been a struggle, and she had never experienced the enjoyment of recreation or relaxation. Now, for the first time, Momma could fully experience the good life.

A smile filled my face as we prepared for our big excursion—we were taking Momma on vacation. Our first stop would be Oklahoma, where my wife's sister Lisa lived. Lisa and her family were delighted to be meeting Momma and had planned some fun outings.

After a long day of driving, we finally arrived. We stepped out of the van as Lisa, her husband, and their children came running out of their house to greet us with welcoming hugs. Lisa had prepared dinner, and after the long drive, we were ready for a good meal. We made our way across the yard to the front entrance, but before stepping into the house, Momma stopped, lifted her dress, and peed in the front yard. Panic overtook me as I fumbled with my words. "Oh my goodness," I thought. "My mother just relieved herself in my sister-in-law's front yard." My wife looked at me, laughed, and said, "Well, she will have to learn that she can't do that in America." Lisa responded through her laughter, "Well, that was some introduction."

It didn't stop there—oh, no! Momma had a few more cultural mishaps during our visit. A nice picnic on the beach turned into a moment of panic as Momma again relieved herself in the midst of sandcastles, children playing, and people picnicking. Jenny and Lisa sprang into action, holding up beach towels to create privacy.

Indoor plumbing was completely foreign to Momma. In Haiti, it was a common practice to urinate in the great outdoors, and she had no idea that such an act in America could land her in jail. She thought nothing of it as she proceeded to pee in a parking lot full of onlookers. Jenny once again jumped in, opening the car door in an effort to block my mother's indecent exposure. Thank the Lord that within a couple of days, Momma caught on to the idea of bathrooms. I guess we could take Momma out of Haiti, but we could not take Haiti out of Momma.

Our next stop was Daytona Beach, Florida, where we stayed in a condo that sat against the blue-green waters of the Atlantic Ocean. It was pure luxury. The white sand continued on for miles as the waves danced along the shore. The dark blue sky was with brilliant white clouds, making for a spectacular day on the beach. Jenny prepared a beach bag and placed a hat on Momma's head while I grabbed lounge chairs and beach umbrellas. The boys grabbed their football, Maddy gathered together sand toys, and we ventured out to the beach for a day of enjoyment and relaxation.

The closer we got to the water, the more my mom hesitated. She stopped, looked at the waves crashing against the shore, and tugged on my arm. She was full of questions. "Why are we here? Are we going to take a bath in the water?"

"No, Momma," I responded. "We're going to swim and relax."

She was completely puzzled; the idea of recreation was beyond her life experiences. She watched as Jenny and I played in the waves, Maddy built sandcastles, and the boys tossed around the football. I teased Momma, splashing her with water and rubbing sand over her feet. She shook her head and grinned. She cautiously observed, spending the afternoon sitting under an umbrella with her feet buried in the sand, taking in this new experience called *vacation*.

There was never a dull moment—Momma's discoveries kept us amused and entertained. One evening, Momma decided to pamper herself with the collection of lotion, soap, and powder that Jenny often shared with her. She meandered into the living room afterwards, wearing her satin pajamas and fuzzy slippers—and covered in white powder. Her ebony face was white like a mime's, and the dusty cloud that trailed behind her as she sauntered over to the couch left white imprints on the floor. We doubled over with laughter as Momma gave us a huge, toothless grin, impressed with her discovery. Powder was everywhere. That day, Momma learned that a little goes a long way.

Another specific memory of Momma continues to keep us laughing. The kids were in the living room one afternoon quietly watching a television program until Momma strolled in wearing a shimmery pink raincoat with four buttons down the front, a fabric belt around the waist, and a bulky, leopard-patterned fur collar. She was fumbling with the buttons but didn't fasten them properly. As she shuffled through the living room, her coat suddenly opened, revealing the outfit underneath: *her birthday suit*!

Our peaceful afternoon was shattered by this jaw-dropping, heart-pounding wardrobe malfunction. Justin and Ben panicked in shock at the sight of their exposed grandmother and covered their eyes, their flustered voices echoing throughout the house. Justin yelled, "Pluck out my eyes!" Ben fell to the floor, covered his head with a pillow, and screamed, "Oh, my gosh!" But thank the Lord for granddaughters. Madisen ran to the rescue, pulling, pushing, adjusting, and finally fixing Momma's catastrophe. The children laughed themselves into a stupor talking about how they never wanted to see Momma in the pink raincoat again.

To this day, I don't know why she was wearing the coat. Perhaps she liked the way it looked, or she thought it was a bathrobe. She had never had many clothing options, and her new choices often confused her.

Momma's first birthday party at the age of seventy-seven also made a lasting impression. Raw emotion poured over her as she beheld her birthday cake, tears running down her face. We were celebrating her life, and the reality that she was important enough to be celebrated overwhelmed her. She sat, her hands raised to the sky, singing and praising God. The realization that a small birthday party could be so significant touched us, and tears streamed down our faces, too. I sat holding her hand, appreciating the moment right along with her. I was honored to celebrate the life of my cherished mom.

Momma's first Christmas in America was overwhelming to her, as she couldn't believe all the blessings. She had never experienced decorating a tree or opening gifts on Christmas morning. Celebrating Christmas in Haiti meant preparing a small portion of food (usually whatever they could scrounge up) and walking several miles barefoot to attend a church service. Momma had no idea there would be such abundance surrounding her. Piles of hot baked rolls, mashed potatoes, turkey, honey-baked ham, and desserts crowded the counters. Momma stood in awe.

Ribbons, wrappings, lights, and gifts were scattered throughout the house. The family gathered around laughing, talking, and enjoying each other's company. Songs and games added to the festivities.

During one game, we all sat in a circle and passed a gift back and forth to a story being told. Each time we heard the word "right," we would pass the gift to the right, and at the word "left," we would pass the gift to the left. The person holding the gift at the end of the story won a prize. Finally, the gift landed in Momma's lap, she picked it up with a big smile and held it in her hand. But as soon as she gripped it, we heard the word "left," and a hand swooped in and grabbed the treasure. Momma immediately got upset, pouting as she watched the gift being tossed from person to person. Watching Momma's reaction, we fumbled with the package and exploded with laughter as the game quickly became a challenge of getting the reward back to Momma. She was like a child, watching with intensity as her eyes focused on it. She was perplexed until finally, the gift landed back in her lap. The prize was a simple chocolate bar, but to Momma it was much more—it represented a fleeting moment of abundance that followed a lifetime of lack.

On another occasion, Momma, nieces, and aunts were gathered around a small coffee table. Karen, Nancy VanHoose's sister, had brought over some of her jewelry to be shared. They quickly picked up and tried on various pieces, and then complimented each other on their trinkets.

Momma sat close to Justin, peering into a box that held several shiny necklaces. She had never owned such glamorous items, and their beauty intrigued her. Justin grabbed one and put it around Momma's neck. "Oui," Momma replied with a huge smile. Delighted that he was pleasing his grandmother, Justin picked up another necklace and placed it around her neck. "Oui," Momma said again. Her eyes were as big as saucers as she held onto the beads that dangled around her neck. It quickly became a game as Justin would nod his head "yes" and say, "Oui Momma." Momma would smile at Justin and say, "Oui." Momma's response encouraged Justin's behavior, and before long, she had a heap of necklaces hanging around her neck. "Okay, Justin, that's enough," Jenny said. Justin just laughed, ignoring his mother's warning.

Before the evening was over, Momma was the queen of bling. She had never seen so much jewelry. She pranced around the room like the belle of the ball, wearing all of the necklaces at once. Thanks to Justin, we left the party with more than twenty of them—all hanging around Momma's neck.

My family had the privilege of learning the life lessons that accompanied Momma's exploration. She brought awareness of Haitian culture and taught us that we are more alike than we are different. Even with a language barrier, our children had no trouble communicating their affection; she knew they loved her, and they knew she loved them. They would laugh, hug, hold hands, and tease one another.

Momma's inner strength could be seen and felt as she explored her new world, unafraid of trying new adventures and creating a lifetime of memories. She transformed our quiet afternoons into images that will be forever etched into our minds. Sharing each moment with Momma as she encountered the abundance of America was inspirational. She stepped out through an opened door and experienced new horizons. Life for her was new each morning, as she was not afraid to live. Momma reached out beyond what she thought was possible and transformed surviving into living.

The first time Bryan went to Haiti, he reunited with Momma and sent Reeser and Jenny this picture. It ws the first time Reeser had seen his mother in over twenty-three years.

2005—Jenny and Momma meeting for the first time at the orphanage.

Jenny and Momma meeting for the first time. Momma is watching video of her grandchildren and her son.

2009—Momma is greeted by family and friends at her big arrival in America.

2010—Momma's first Christmas in America with her grandchildren.
(from left to right: Justin, Ben, and Maddy)

Reeser with his adoptive mom and birth mom.

2014—Reeser and Jenny leading worship at The Cathedral.

The Williams Family
Jenny, Justin, Ben, Maddy, and Reeser

Faith, Hope, and Love

Jeremiah 29:11 says, "For I know the thoughts that I think toward you, says the Lord, thoughts of peace and not of evil, to give you a future and a hope." Looking back over my life, it is easy to see the hand of the Lord guiding me and carrying me through the impossible. Not only did He give me hope in a hopeless situation, but He also gave me a future.

It's only fitting that I quote from the song, *You've Been Faithful*, by Eddie James. The inspired words say it all, which is why I have made it my life anthem:

As I look back over my life
I can see how Your love has guided me
Even though I've done wrong
You've never left me alone
But You forgave me
And You kept on blessing
This I recall to my mind
Therefore I have hope
It's because of Your mercy that we are not consumed
Because thy compassions fail not,
They are new every morning
Great is Your faithfulness
Great is Your faithfulness

I can never repay you Lord for what You've done for me
How You loosed my shackles and You set me free.
How You made a way out of no way

Turned my darkness into day
You've been my joy in the time of sorrow
Hope for my tomorrow
Peace in the time of storm
Strength when I'm weak and worn.

You've been, Lord, You've been so faithful[v]

It's been a journey—a hold-onto-your-restraints, rocky, wild, adventurous journey. At times I had no idea where I would live, what I would eat, if my tumor would take my life, or what uncertainty would be around the corner. There were many situations that I couldn't control, but I learned quickly that I could change the way I responded to and perceived the circumstances. I lived in Haiti, but the hardship of Haiti didn't have to live in me. Discovering my passion, staying persistent, and allowing God to define me was the key to my success.

My life has become more than I could have imagined or dreamed. I've come to appreciate the obstacles I've faced and conquered, since each hardship and victory has strengthened me. I'm thankful for every opportunity presented to me that has freed me from the grip of poverty and death. Most of all, I'm grateful for the outpourings of love I've received.

My life is a true testament of His powerful love—love that conquered death and transformed me from a poor orphan to an *orphan with a crown*. It is a title I wear with pride.

Notes

---

[i]VanHoose, A. D., with Rod Spence. 1983. "Conversation with an Angel" and "The Answered Prayer." In *I Met an Angel*, The Reverend A. D. VanHoose, 79-84 and 116-117. Detroit: Harlo Press.
[ii]VanHoose and Rod Spence. "Papa Doc," 129-134.
[iii]http://www.songlyrics.com/gaither-vocal-band/he-touched-me-lyrics/, accessed June 12, 2020.
[iv]www.visualgeography.com/countries/haiti.html, accessed September 29, 2020.
[v]https://www.azlyrics.com/lyrics/eddiejames/youvebeensofaithful.html, accessed December 5, 2020.

www.reejenministries.com
Visit our website for a free mp3 download of "You've Been So Faithful"